Reader comments about 'I also by Andy Zipser

From Amazon:

Andy is a straight shooter
A very interesting read. Goes straight to the heart of what it is like to be an owner/operator of an RV campground. This was especially interesting to me because I had stayed at Andy's campground at least three times while he was the owner. It's a job I could never do because they have to put up with too much BS from (clueless) customers. —*Merlin Billings*

Very Relatable
Having owned a B&B these stories are so relatable. Very well written and easy to follow and enjoy. Fun read!—*Anthony Barthel*

A great book about business and the changing face of camping
This book is a really good look at how a family pursued its dream of owning a campground, and why they decided to sell it years later. If you've ever sat and dreamed about starting or buying a business based on your passion, read this book. It's well written and worth your time. It's also an interesting look at the business of camping from the inside, which most campers and RVers may not know.—*T. Kates*

From GoodReads:

What I expected to read was a look at running an RV park/resort/campground with light-hearted reports on interacting with RVers but what I got was a fairly serious look at the business side of working with a KOA franchise. I wasn't disappointed as it was an interesting and eye-opening look at what goes on behind the scenes. He also went into how the pandemic affected his resort and how they found ways to keep making a profit.—*Robin*

This quick read offered an interesting, albeit negative, tale of campground ownership. If you have an itch to operate a campground, these 128 pages will scratch it without depleting your life's savings. Interesting, educational, and enjoyable.—*Matthew*

"So take note when you see dirt turned. Thank the turner for starting something. Thank you for turning dirt everyday. Who knows, you might hit pay dirt."

—*Bob Schaller, Dept. of Economic Development, St. Mary's County, MD*

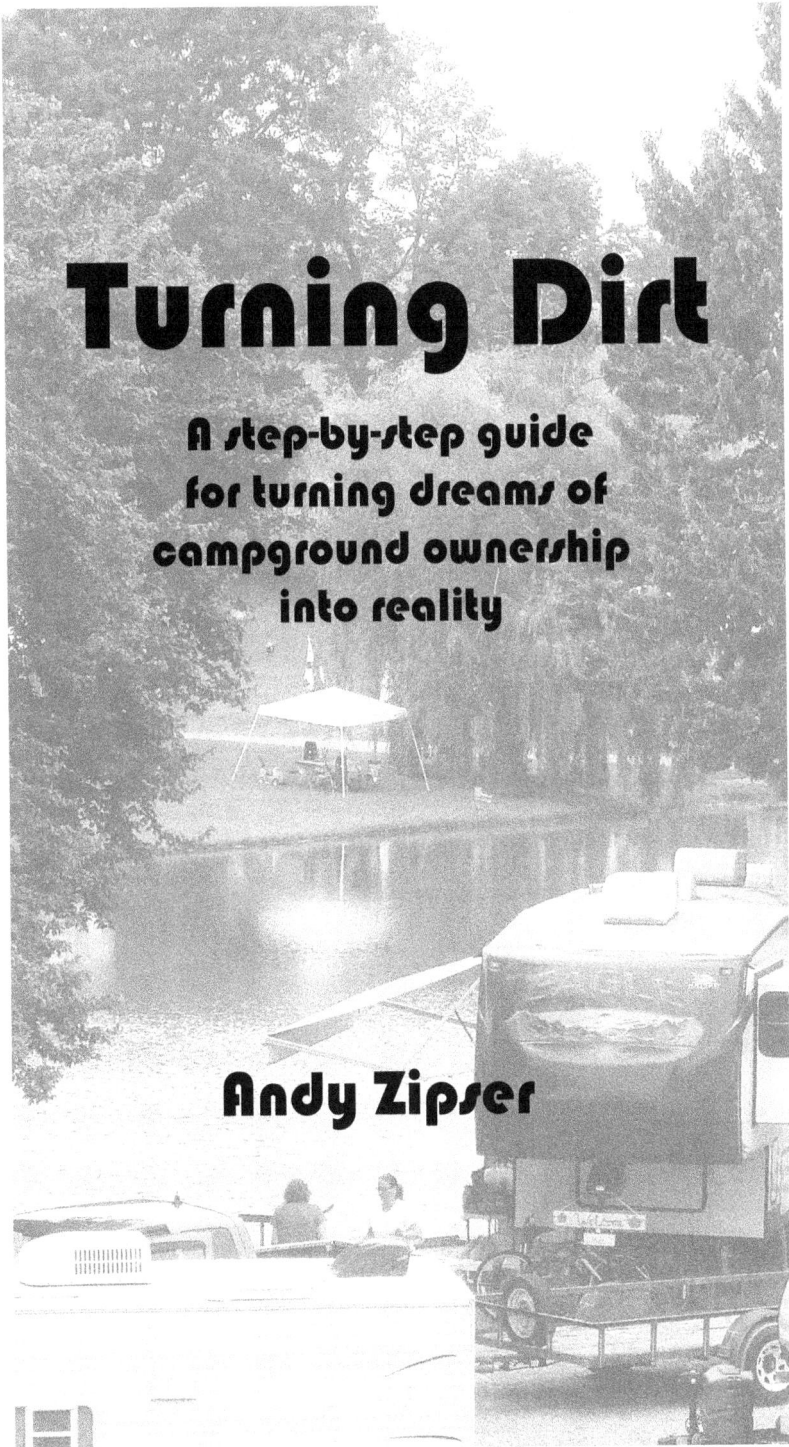

Turning Dirt

A step-by-step guide
for turning dreams of
campground ownership
into reality

Andy Zipser

The contents of this book are provided for information purposes only and do not constitute legal or financial advice. Anyone intent on purchasing commercial property is strongly encouraged to consult with a real estate attorney and a tax accountant licensed in the state in which the property is located, as tax, incorporation and other relevant laws will vary from one jurisdiction to another.

The author will appreciate receiving any corrections or additions to the material in this book.

All communications may be directed to:
azipser@renting-dirt.com

ISBN: 978-1-7377750-2-7 (Paperback)
ISBN: 978-1-7377750-3-4 (eBook)

Library of Congress Control Number: 2022909289

Published by Mint Spring Publishing, Mint Spring, VA
Printed in the United States of America, 2022.

Table of Contents

Getting down to business

Introduction

LAST YEAR I WROTE A BOOK titled *Renting Dirt*, which I thought was a darn catchy description of the business my family was in for eight years, that of running a mid-sized campground in the Shenandoah Valley. It got good reader reviews and had decent sales, especially given my completely unfunded marketing efforts. And it prompted me to start a blog about RVs and the campground industry that very slowly but steadily has gained some traction.

So why this sequel? What's different from the original?

The answer to the first question is that I've been asked too many times why I had written *Renting Dirt* in the first place. Who was it written for? Was it merely a cathartic exercise, an expunging of demons so I could move on with the rest of my life? Was I just settling scores? Was there nothing even remotely satisfying about the eight years our family ran Walnut Hills Campground and RV Park?

And the answers to those questions are that a) I basically wrote the book for myself; b) it *was* cathartic; and c) it wasn't a matter of settling scores as much as an attempt to even things out—to throw up a counterweight to all the rah-rah boosterism that afflicts this business, a splash of ice water to cool down the fever that so often grips the aspiring entrepreneurs (me included) who stumble into this line of work. And *of course* there were good times. No sane person would keep at the same all-consuming effort for eight years without an occasional surge of pride and sense of accomplishment. It's just that those moments were too few and far between.

Nonetheless, some readers made it clear that they didn't get a big charge from reading an unremitting critique, regardless of how briskly written it might be. Then there's the problem of my original subtitle: "An unfertilized (no BS) look at what it takes to run a campground and RV park." To the extent that this set up the expectation of a "how-to" guide, it could have been better crafted.

Maybe something along the lines of, "How running a campground can run you into the ground," or "Renting dirt is a dirty business, so be prepared to get soiled." Or . . . well, you get the idea.

The reality is that there are very few how-to books on buying or operating RV campgrounds, and the handful out there are either outdated or superficial, rattling on about general small business practices (make sure you get liability insurance/know your target audience/keep accurate financial records, etc. etc.) without ever delving into the peculiarities of managing, you know—campgrounds. To the extent that readers desperate to know more about the business picked up *Renting Dirt* because they were looking for tips and pointers they weren't getting elsewhere, they may have been disappointed.

That's why this new book, *Turning Dirt*, as in "tilling the soil," as in making something more productive. This time I'm writing not for myself or my friends (or, to be frank, for other campground owners, who almost universally were nodding their heads knowingly as they read my account) but for you, my imagined reader. The person fixed in my mind's eye as I write the next 45,000 or so words, eyes widening with surprise or brows knitted in concentration as I relate, describe, prescribe and warn about the many, many things you're better off knowing before plunging into the campground morass.

In my mind's eye you almost certainly have some, if not necessarily a lot, of RVing experience, and you've been wondering what it would take to actually own one of the places you've stayed at. If you've already read *Renting Dirt*, you haven't been deterred—a testament either to your self-confidence or your bullheadedness, either of which will be crucial to your success as you plunge ahead. But whether you've read *Renting Dirt* or not, you're looking for pointers and signposts, advice and cautions, red flags and green lights. You want to know the things I wish I'd known before getting into this business, and that's what this book is about.

Unlike *Renting Dirt*, which presented an unvarnished account of our family's experience as campground owners, *Turning Dirt* is agnostic on just about everything. My purpose is not to have you view something from a certain perspective, or to convince you of one thing or another, but simply to lay out the steps I think you should take to arrive at a thoughtful decision about the big step you're contemplating. The issues I raise and the process I describe are based not only on my eight years as a campground owner, but on my ongoing engagement with the industry as a critical observer and writer, both for my own blog and for the online magazine RVtravel. It is, in other words, an informed presentation—but it isn't gospel. Take what's valuable or insightful, set aside the rest and forge your own path.

The ten chapters that follow are laid out in three progressive sections. The first, "Establishing the Basics," describes how much the industry has changed over the past decade due to several factors—the pandemic is only one of several—and how that affects both the marketplace and your opportunities within it. This section goes on to explore your motivation and goals, then finishes by presenting several major choices that will help you narrow your search for the "right" campground.

The second section, "Finding and Buying What You Want," is exactly what it sounds like: a step-by-step description of how to structure your search, how to assess your various prospects and how to take the plunge of making an offer. The last chapter in this section describes the steps you'll have to take from the moment both parties reach agreement to the actual closing date. Moreover, this section is supplemented by three appendices at the end of the book, providing a sample offer letter, a due diligence checklist and an overview of the main elements of a purchase agreement.

Finally, the third section, "Getting Down to Business," explores the initial operational choices and decisions you'll be facing, including your employees, your guests, your rates and fees and your various campground policies. It also touches on various subjects that are unique—or almost so—to campground operations, from bed bugs and golf cars to automatic external defibrillators and why employees should be trained in using them.

Throughout, I've tried to stay focused on those issues and

decision points that are unique to the campground industry. This is not a general guide to best business practices, and presupposes that you either have a general understanding of how to operate a generic business or know how to get that education elsewhere. So, for example, *Turning Dirt* does not get into Small Business Administration loans as a possible funding source, does not discuss bookkeeping, and ignores social media and reviews, all of which are important and all of which are subjects with which you'll be engaging, but all of which are common to any contemporary business.

There are plenty of other things unique to campgrounds and RV parks to learn about—plenty enough to fill this book, as you'll see—without getting sidetracked.

Establishing the basics

Chapter 1:
Everything Is Different Today

BEFORE WE GET INTO THE BASICS of what it takes to find, buy and operate an RV park and campground, I think it's important for you to understand how and why this moment is quite unlike any other. I can guarantee that almost anything you've read or seen about camping, RVs, and RV parks is already out-dated, thanks to a crush of recent developments—from the pandemic to climate change to the blossoming of institutional investment interest—that are rapidly reshaping the industry landscape.

This book is being written in the first half of 2022, or roughly ten years after my wife and I decided we were going to buy an RV campground. Back then, the notion that we would sell almost all our worldly possessions, cash out my pension plan and plow everything we had into buying a campground was still a vaguely loony idea. We were urban dwellers, a population that largely viewed camping as a quirky, fringe activity in the same category as bowling or square dancing.

Meanwhile, any business associated with recreational vehicles had gone off a cliff after the Great Recession of 2007-2008, which took a bite out of RV sales, campground revenues and everything in between. The public perception of RVing was either that of families with small kids out for a weekend in a small pop-up or travel trailer, or of old folks cruising America's highways in motorhomes or pulling large fifth-wheels with bumper stickers reading, "We're spending our kids' inheritances." Serious people didn't see a future in betting the bank on such an unpredictable and cash-strapped customer base.

But years earlier, we—perhaps like you—had spent time camping with our younger daughter. The three of us, and sometimes one of our daughter's friends, would roll around the Midwest and up into Canada in a borrowed Class C, spending two to three weeks exploring as far west as Devil's Tower and as far east as the Bay of Fundy. We went as the spirit moved us, rarely planning more than a day ahead, always finding a campground for the night and sometimes, on the spur of the moment, extending our stay by two or three days.

We found warm and hospitable people everywhere we went (well, except for one particular run-in at the Canadian border, when I burst out laughing in response to being asked if we were carrying any firearms; apparently that was no laughing matter, earning us a special half-hour's attention). We made numerous unexpected discoveries, the memory of which—like the House on the Rock—linger to this day. We grew closer as a family and finished each trip relaxed and rejuvenated.

Those were fun times, fondly remembered, and if they somewhat parallel your own experience, I understand how strongly nostalgia has pulled you into thinking how great it would be to have a campground of your own. It also doesn't help that there's a whole mini industry of "insiders," some of whom already may have been whispering in your ear, promoting the idea that owning a campground is the most incredibly rewarding way to make a living short of developing penicillin. Consider, for example, the author of a book about his experiences who wrote, just a couple of years ago, "As someone who owns an RV park, I must tell you it is so much fun I would do it for free. . . . There are few other business ventures where you can dedicate your days to having fun."

Or consider the blandishments of Frank Rolfe, the talkative half of the duo behind a dubious operation calling itself RV Park University, a subject to which I'll return later. He regularly issues blast emails promoting campground ownership that stress a) how little work goes into operating paradise, and b) how much fun it all is. One such effort in 2021, for example, was headlined,

"Vacation while you work: welcome to the RV park owner's life-style." The text went on to elaborate that "you have the best of both worlds" when owning an RV park because this "will allow you to effectively feel like you're on vacation while you're working."

If something sounds too good to be true . . .

If something sounds too good to be true, I hope you've had enough life experience to understand it probably is—and if you don't know that yet, my advice is that you reconsider going into business for yourself. Hyping anything as worthy of your attention because it's "fun" or like being on vacation is Tom Sawyer getting his friends to whitewash Aunt Polly's fence. Owning a campground? It's always been a lot of work, and even more so in recent years. Fun? Sometimes—but if that's your primary motivation, you're better off looking elsewhere.

There's one notable exception to that observation: if you're part of an investment group that's looking at campgrounds and RV parks as the next hot commercial real estate niche, then buying, owning and ultimately selling an RV campground is "fun" in the same way that an afternoon playing Monopoly can be fun. For that person, campgrounds are fungible assets no different than self-storage warehouses or trailer parks—both, not incidentally, also part of Frank Rolfe's portfolio. They're interchangeable and abstract, their attractiveness measured solely in terms of net operating income and cap rates, and when they disappoint are readily replaced by the next alluring investment.

Odds are, however, that you're not in that category—not if you're reading this book. Odds are that you, like my wife, Carin, and me in the early days, are thinking about sinking your life savings into a property you hope will provide a decent income and possibly a place to live. Maybe you're thinking that a campground will be a side gig—a business you can oversee on the weekends while you keep your regular 9-5. Or maybe you're thinking that it could be the start of a family business, one you can pass on to your kids. Or you're about to retire but aren't ready to quit working. Whatever it is, you're not thinking about taking on an assignment that will eat up your every waking hour, suck you dry emotionally and work you twice as hard as any job you've had until now.

If, that is, you intend to do a good job of it.

As with any generalization, there are exceptions—and, indeed, there are campgrounds that illustrate it's possible to avoid the burdens of ownership. Carin and I would refer to those as examples of inmates running the asylum, and if you've been poking around, you've probably encountered a few of these. It's not just that the grounds and buildings appear neglected, the former long on grass and the latter short on paint. It's that there appear to be no rules or standards. Vehicles park anywhere and everywhere, even if that means ruts, potholes and broken brush. Long-term sites are marked by add-on porches, outbuildings and appliances stashed outside, all in various states of disrepair; short-term sites are overrun with weeds and littered with cigarette butts. Loud gatherings continue until the early morning hours, campfires blazing and music echoing throughout the surrounding area.

Some of these campgrounds can exude a faint air of menace, while others are simply annoying. Carin and I have driven through eerily quiet campgrounds at 11 in the morning and realized we were being eyed from behind drawn curtains as we rolled by, as if we were revenue agents looking for the next still. We've also stayed at an apparently high-dollar property in which teenagers were whooping it up while drag-racing golf cars after midnight, not a hundred feet from our travel trailer, with apparently no one on hand to put a lid on things. Either way, it's clear that rules at such campgrounds—if any—are readily disregarded because no one is around to enforce them.

Rule number one: you have to be there

All of which is to say that the first rule of successful campground ownership is: YOU HAVE TO BE THERE. All the time. And if it's not you personally, it had better be someone you trust and whom you've empowered to do what it takes, up to and including ejection of campers, to enforce your rules and maintain order. We know a couple who lived in Tennessee, bought a campground near Des Moines, and thought they could run the latter from home while they continued with their regular jobs. That lasted less than a year before they realized what a colossal misunderstanding that had been, at which point they quit their jobs, moved to Iowa and transformed their acquisition into one of the highest-rated franchises in the KOA system. But that took commitment. And hard work.

Contrast that with another couple we know who bought a campground in Georgia and were lucky enough to inherit an extraordinary pair of managers who had already been working there 18 months. That stroke of good luck enabled the buyers to continue living in the Atlanta area for the next nine years, continuing in their regular jobs, with the wife maintaining the books and taking care of the campground's web presence and marketing from home, while her husband would drive down every two weekends or so for some of the bigger maintenance jobs. "Those days were really fun," the wife told me—until the day the managers "just up and hit the road early one Sunday morning," with no warning and no explanation. After trying various management approaches over the next couple of years, the owners finally decided they wanted out and sold the place.

Finding good employees to work in a campground has always been difficult, and is something I'll explore more in Chapter 7. Suffice for now to say that the Great Resignation plaguing the hospitality sector in general has been doubly hard on campgrounds and RV parks, if only because so many of them were already at a hiring disadvantage because they can't offer year-round employment in a seasonal business. Meanwhile, the amount of business that this depleted workforce has to serve has exploded—also because of the pandemic—as a public weary of social distancing and quarantining realized there is no better cocoon than an RV: sleep in your own bed, have exclusive use of a bathroom unsullied by the masses, cook your own food and eat from your own dishes—and all this while traveling anywhere in the country you want to go.

And it's not just vacationing. As the pandemic drove millions out of office buildings to work from home, the realization dawned that working "remotely" could mean working from anywhere that has a decent wifi connection. And just like that, huge swaths of Millennials and Gen-Xers took to RVs like lemmings to the sea, to such an extent that they now constitute a third of the customer base. Move over, grandma and grandpa!

But while this might seem like a favorable development—who wouldn't want more business? —there are two key things to keep in mind. First, unlike a decade ago, most campgrounds are running at or uncomfortably close to 100% capacity, which means there's little upside left for the new buyer. If you acquire a campground with 30% or 45% occupancy, the selling price should be correspondingly lower than it would be for the same campground operating at 60% or 90% occupancy; moreover, you now have room to increase business, which means more cash flow and, ultimately, a more valuable piece of property. (That's one reason, incidentally, why the creepy campground with tenants peeking out from behind their curtains could be an excellent purchase—if you're capable of cleaning them out and upgrading the property.) Increased business benefits existing campground owners more than prospective ones.

In with the new, out with the old

Second, the increased business of just the past few years has resulted in a huge cultural shift. All those RV newbies—11 million of them in just the past few years—are jumping in with both feet with little if any prior preparation. That has practical consequences, from not knowing how to use utility hook-ups to being starkly inept at backing their (often massive) new rolling homes into an RV site, resulting in smashed fences, hydrants and power pedestals, or sewage flowing out of shut-off valves because, well, isn't every PVC pipe in the ground there to receive a black tank's contents?

That bull-in-a-china-shop syndrome means a lot more work for campground owners, at least for now, while the newbies get on-the-job training. But the extent to which all those new RVers can rearrange the landscape pales beside the roughshod way they can—and often do—run over traditional campground practices, many of which revolve around unspoken rules: don't cut through other campers' sites, don't use fire rings as trash receptacles, don't leave outside lights on all night, pick up after your dog, don't go knocking on another RVer's door except in a true emergency, and on and on. A lot of these proscriptions have to do with issues of personal space, which is much more vulnerable to intrusion in an environment of thin-walled dwellings parked cheek-by-jowl with each other. But many also grow out of the individualistic and often libertarian leanings that many old-school RVers embody—leanings that the preponderance of newer RVers don't share and often don't even recognize.

If that sounds a bit abstract, here's a simpler way to put it: a huge percentage of today's new RVers are fundamentally hotel guests who happen to have brought their hotel rooms with them. They expect hotel types of amenities, demand a hotel-level of service and attention and treat other RVers like other hotel guests, which is to say, as strangers who might have to be stepped around. That isn't just my perception—it's a phenomenon long-term campground owners across the country have observed, often with a tinge of sadness and always with some frustration, because the new campers have negated a lot of the "fun" that once made campground ownership more personally rewarding. They're often more aloof, more demanding, more entitled and less forgiving, and they've helped turn this into more of a transactional relationship than it used to be—although as we'll see later, they didn't do that by themselves.

But there's more than a pandemic-driven increase in business and its resulting cultural dislocation that makes campground ownership in 2022 so hugely different. If you're seriously thinking about making this your new life's work, you need to consider three other external developments that are having an outsized effect on the industry: climate change, corporate investment and growing social wariness toward "gasoline gypsies."

Climate change, big money and ski runs

Did your neck hairs bristle when I mentioned climate change? Would it help if I used the phrase "extreme weather"? Because whatever your politics—it's unfortunate that everything has become so politicized that even the weather can be a partisan issue—it's an undeniable fact that extreme weather is battering the countryside with increased frequency and severity. And while RVers with an ear to the ground can pack up and haul ass before their lightweight and extraordinarily flammable rolling shelters get slammed about by a tornado or derecho, or melted into a slag pile by a forest or grassland fire, any campground you buy will be rooted in place.

One predictable result is a growing list of campgrounds that have been closed for up to three years as they rebuild from being ravaged by increasingly devastating natural forces, from forest fires in the west to hurricanes along the Gulf Coast to flooding from overflowing rivers just about anywhere. Acknowledging that trend should be a major factor when deciding what campground to purchase, as I'll discuss more in Chapter 3, but also has other implications, such as insurance rates and provisions for camper safety. For example, there now are many more campgrounds in "tornado alley" that build—and heavily advertise—underground bunkers in which their customers can shelter as needed.

Corporate investment—a phrase I'm using loosely, since a lot of the money now sloshing into the campground sector is coming from investors and speculators who don't operate under a corporate umbrella—is another recent development that has significantly altered industry dynamics, both in acquisitions and operationally. A decade ago, corporate ownership of campgrounds was a mere blip on the screen, with even the very largest campgrounds in the country owned by families who had built and expanded them over three or four generations. As an industry, campgrounds were too small, too arcane and too primitive operationally to attract big-money investors.

That started changing, however, just about the time we bought our campground in 2013. Sun Outdoors, for example—now one of the biggest players in the industry—acquired its first Jellystone campground that same year. Today, in addition to owning more than a dozen additional Jellystone franchises, it also owns Leisure Systems Inc., the company that licenses the Jellystone name and its Hanna Barbera characters to nearly 90 properties across the country.

Having companies like Sun, Northgate, Equity Lifestyle Properties, Blue Water and even KOA—once focused almost entirely on franchising its name, but which has been acquiring its own properties at an increasing tempo—sniffing around at properties that you might also be considering obviously puts you at a competitive disadvantage. Most of the big money currently isn't interested in campgrounds smaller than 200 sites or so, but as the industry consolidates and the larger attractive properties get snapped up, that threshold will drop. The result is spiraling prices, higher costs and a dwindling number of independent owners.

In that respect, campgrounds are following the same developmental arc once traced by ski runs, now almost exclusively transformed into ski resorts. As recounted by Peter Pelland, a skiing enthusiast who primarily designs websites for family-owned campgrounds, the "golden age" of skiing occurred in the 1950s, when literally hundreds of mom-and-pop operations dotted New England's hills and mountains, their rope tows powered by tractors and old Packard automobile engines. But then the ski resort "industry" started gobbling them up and throwing money around, and by 1975 there were only 745 ski areas left—throughout the entire United States. That number dropped to 509 by 2000, and then 470 by 2020, and as it did, the cost for a day on the slopes climbed into the hundreds of dollars per skier.

How this dynamic evolves is not a mystery—it's already started in the campground industry, with the surge of new "hotel-type" campers bringing their non-traditional, higher expectations. It's visible also at conferences and conventions of campground owners, whether hosted by KOA or Jellystone for their franchisees, or the National Association of RV Parks and Campgrounds, the only nationwide campground trade group. At these affairs, the shining example repeatedly held up for campground owners to emulate is the Walt Disney Company, extolled for its obsessive attention to detail, hospitality and "the guest experience."

While all that may be worth examining—and there's more of that in Chapter 8—what's relevant here is to observe that Disney, like the ski resorts, has transitioned from an everyman holiday destination to a playground for the wealthy and a once-in-a-lifetime bucket list destination for everyone else: the baseline cost for a family of four on a typical 3-4 day Disney vacation now comes in at more than $5,000. Or as observed in late 2021 by Len Testa, president of a travel website, "One day at Disney World—with a hotel and food and everything—costs either as much as or more than 80% of what American households spend on vacations any given year."

RVs as the lowest-cost housing alternative

It's therefore ironic that a fifth trend making 2022 so vastly different from just a decade earlier is occurring at the opposite end of the economic spectrum: the growing flood of RVs—which, remember, is an acronym for *Recreational* Vehicles—that are being repurposed as full-time housing, or *Residential* Vehicles.

The Rving crowd always has included some proportion of full-timers, although estimates vary and there are no hard numbers. Many traditional full-timers may be houseless—notably among the older generation—declaring that they've traded in their sticks-and-bricks dwellings for mobile ones; others may spend much but not all their time in an RV, as is true of "snowbirds" who transition with the seasons from homes in the north to RV campgrounds in the south. But thanks to a growing shortage of affordable housing across the United States, the number of people becoming full-timers out of necessity, not choice, has mushroomed.

I'll discuss that development in a little more detail in Chapter 8, but what makes it relevant here is the effect it has had on the wider public perception of RVs and Rvers. The sight of rattle-trap RVs and vans squatting on city streets or in commercial parking lots, their owners' possessions often strewed across the pavement, has resurrected decades-old fears and revulsion that first surfaced in the Great Depression. Travel trailers were still a relatively new invention at the time, but as mass production lowered costs and a growing number of Americans were thrown out of work, many turned to them as homes of last resort. Dubbed "gasoline gypsies" by the *New Republic*—playing off a derogatory reference to the nomadic Roma people in Europe—the wheeled homeless provoked alarm and suspicion among their more established neighbors, who responded with exclusionary zoning and ordinances.

Much the same dynamic is unfolding today, as municipal officials across the country contend with mounting complaints of drug abuse, theft, panhandling and unsanitary practices. More broadly, however, today's gasoline gypsies are tarnishing the overall image of all RVers, breathing new life into ancient fears of "the traveler." Regardless of how well-heeled they may be, RVers are regarded as transients, not rooted to the local community, here one day and gone the next without any long-term accountability for what they've done locally.

What that means for you as a prospective campground owner is increased community resistance to new campgrounds of almost any size, as well as greater opposition to any plans for expanding an existing facility. Under these circumstances, the most trouble-free RV park acquisition is of an existing property that won't require new variances or other public consideration.

None of this is intended to dissuade you from pursuing your dreams of campground ownership, but rather to puncture the nostalgia balloon that may have brought you to this point and to place your ambitions within a realistic context. What you may have experienced as an RVer in years past is not the RVing world of today, and what you may have read or discussed with people in the business as recently as three or four years ago is likewise dated—and, in some cases, obsolete. Once you understand and accept that, you'll be ready to move on.   ☙

Chapter 2:
Know Thyself

A GOOD STARTING POINT for this exploration of campground ownership is the "why" of it all. I don't mean the "push" factors that may be motivating you, like a desire to escape a dead-end job, or a major life upheaval like divorce or the death of a child. I mean the "pull" factors that put you on this particular trajectory. Of all the possible things you could be contemplating, why campground ownership?

I can think of several possibilities. Most common, I suspect, is the one I raised in the first chapter: you've camped in the past, you remember those excursions fondly, and you hope to recapture those feelings by having a campground of your very own. It should go without saying that being a guest at a campground for a relatively short time, where you have no real responsibilities beyond meeting your own needs, is a world away from owning a business in which you have to attend to the needs of hundreds of paying customers for month after month, in good weather and foul, while also contending with all of the overhead demands of operating any small business. It shouldn't go without saying—and yet it's easy to lose sight of.

I know, because I've been there. I remember being asked repeatedly by one of our campers why I'd willingly take on such a responsibility, because he also operated a small business and had an eye for the complexities of such an undertaking. He was unabashedly disbelieving in my foolishness, but I was still so new to the business that I didn't really appreciate his concern. It took me a couple of years to get there, at which point I hit upon an analogy that most aptly sums things up: just because I enjoy a good steak doesn't mean I should be a cattle rancher. You might think about that for yourself.

But it could be that none of that is true for you. It may be that you've never camped, or have camped only rarely, but you've been seduced by all the recent press about this great "new" niche in the commercial real estate sector. You have some money, maybe from an inheritance or because you've sold another business, and you're looking to put it to work. Or you don't have a lot of money but you have assets that could be liquidated—a home, a pension plan, a boat you wish you'd never bought, a second home—and you're thinking you'd like to consolidate all that into one neat, life-sustaining package.

Or perhaps you've had it with commuting and wasting such a big chunk of your life between home and work. Perhaps you've been working for other people all your life and are tired of conforming to dress codes, navigating the intricacies of a corporate culture, working set hours and resenting the contortions required to also maintain a family life or spousal relationship. You want to be your own boss, and a campground sounds like a bitchin' way to do that!

There are lots of reasons why you may have arrived at this point, so it might be reassuring—or possibly disconcerting—to learn that no matter the reason, you're far from unique. Campground brokers and various industry groups hold regular "new owners" workshops for people who are in exactly the same frame of mind as you are. And over the past couple of years those workshops have been inundated with record numbers of wannabe owners and investors, all chafing to do what you're contemplating.

Here's the dangerous part. Hovering around the fringes of this upswell is a small but increasingly active cottage industry of self-promoters talking up the attractions of campground ownership—and, of course, the services and advice they can offer to help you attain your dreams. As with any sales pitch, you'll hear a lot of emphasis on the upside and little to none on the down. If you listen to these blandishments with an uncritical mind, you'll get the same distorted view that afflicts those who lean on nostalgia and blinkered memory—which is to say, you'll wake up one morning, a couple of years hence, and wonder, "What was I thinking?" The people who push these stories aren't malevolent, but it's crucial you remember that their interests aren't necessarily aligned with yours. They're like the folks who made money in the gold rush by selling shovels and pickaxes, gold pans and sluice mats, and it's to their benefit to encourage you to buy everything they stock, whether you actually need it or not.

If this is how you've been roped in, you'll soon learn that the sales pitch usually will fall into one of two categories, hyping either the high end of the market or the low. But high or low, the primary inducement is that campground ownership is a good way to make a lot of money; any other benefits are purely secondary.

For some, it's all about the Benjamins

An example of the high road is Heather Blankenship, who over the past decade has transformed herself from the owner of a mid-sized campground in Tennessee to a nation-stumping RV industry investor and guru. Her various courses on campground acquisition and management, consisting largely of videos and printed materials, start at just under $1,000—although she does have a couple of teasers that get you in the door for around $200—and run all the way up to $6,000 for a "transformative three-month journey" that includes three one-on-one coaching calls and live group sessions.

Blankenship's pitch is that she's seeking "high-achieving real estate investors looking to break into the RV Park asset class" so you can "unlock the highest investment returns of your life." There's a lot more of that kind of language and an earnest embrace of FIRE, an investment philosophy popularized a decade ago among millennials that stands for "financial independence, retire early." What it boils down to is buying properties that can be improved enough—either because they were distressed initially, or through expansion—to justify substantial rate increases that generate enough cash flow to underwrite additional improvements, and so on and on in a virtuous cycle. Such "forced appreciation" will enable you either to refinance, freeing up capital to invest in a second campground, or to kick back and simply enjoy your enhanced cash flow.

There's nothing wrong with this perspective—as long as you understand that it requires an attitude that has nothing to do with "camping" or "the outdoors." Breaking "into the RV Park asset class" puts campgrounds in the same category as apartment buildings or self-storage facilities: pieces of commercial real estate designed to house people or things while extracting as much cash as the market will bear, and that's a long way from a misty-eyed pining for campfires and s'mores. It requires more money up-front than other approaches to campground ownership, because as Blankenship correctly notes, it's harder to kick-start smaller parks; and it doesn't leave much room for conceits about life-work balance. But if that's the way you want to roll, you've got lots of company: when Blankenship held an hour-long webinar in late 2021 to pitch her services, more than 1,500 people signed on.

For others, bottom-feeding is the lure

Where Blankenship is aiming for the high end of the market, the grandly named RV Park University and its founders, Dave Reynolds and Frank Rolfe, are unabashedly fixated on the low—unsurprisingly so, since the bulk of their investing has been in mobile home parks, usually referred to as trailer courts. And there, the guiding philosophy has been to raise rates repeatedly but to decrease amenities, thereby increasing revenues while cutting expenses. Such a cut-throat approach works in trailer parks because their residents are mostly trapped: their "mobile" homes usually aren't mobile at all, either because they're too old to be moved or because moving them is too expensive, so their owners have few options. Most RV owners, on the other hand, don't have that limitation: raise rates too high or cut amenities too much and you'll lose your customers. Or so it would seem.

One offsetting factor is a category of recreational "vehicles," known as park models, that increasingly look less like vehicles and more like conventional manufactured housing. Built on single chassis trailers, park models are cabins that can be up to 14 feet wide and include "lofts" up to five feet high, virtually amounting to a second story. Most don't have holding tanks, so need a water and sewer connection to use the plumbing, and typically have their wheels and tongues removed at setup so the whole thing can be skirted to conceal the undercarriage. But because they're limited to 400 square feet of enclosed floor space, park models are exempted from federal housing standards, even as they're promoted by the industry as suitable for year-round living—and a growing number of people are doing just that.

Park models, it should be evident, often are no more mobile than their larger trailer park cousins, leaving their owners at least somewhat captive. But even greater mobility doesn't necessarily translate into greater freedom of movement. Because of the recent explosion in campground occupancy rates, RV owners able to hit the road easily may find they have no place to go—or at least no place where they can stay for more than a few days. Couple that with the increased demand for RV sites overall, and campground owners have encountered markedly reduced resistance to price increases or service cutbacks.

Given those marketplace developments and a blurring distinction between trailer courts and RV parks, Reynolds and Rolfe have shifted some of their attention to the latter. But rather than hype the high intensity "forced appreciation" approach counseled by Blankenship, the duo promotes a two-pronged sales pitch that emphasizes the joys of RV park ownership ("They're a lot of fun. Many of them can feel like a big backyard barbeque.") on one hand, and on the other stresses the rewards of raising rates, both directly and indirectly (start charging long-term guests for water and trash removal), while slashing costs (getting rid of costly amenities like swimming pools). Like Blankenship, they do so via a series of CDs, videos, manuals and other online resources they value at $4,688 but which—hold your horses! —can be purchased from RV Park University for just under $500.

Again, there's nothing "wrong" with this approach, even though it amounts to exploitative bottom-fishing. But it is another example of how campground ownership can have little to do with camping or Mother Nature, and if all you're after is a place to put your money in hopes of getting a 10% annual return, either one of these promoters will be eager to show you how. Just be on the lookout for snake oil.

Do your research

Let's proceed, though, on the assumption that this is not why you're thinking about buying a campground. Sure, you want a return on your investment, but there are other rewards you're after as well—intangible, off balance-sheet rewards, like being your own boss, working outdoors at a variety of tasks that challenge both mind and body, integrating your personal and working lives, building an enterprise you can pass on to your children—all things, incidentally, that someone like Frank Rolfe hypes mercilessly, if superficially.

In other words, if you're after something a little more complex than is provided by a one-dimensional "investment" view of campgrounds, you'll have to start educating yourself about the different possibilities. What looks from a distance like one undifferentiated mass known as "campgrounds" resolves, at closer inspection, into a huge variety of different facilities all lumped under one label. There are campgrounds and there are RV parks—what's the difference? There are long-term campgrounds and transient campgrounds, destination parks and overnight parks, seasonal and year-round campgrounds, membership parks, clothing-optional parks, franchised campgrounds and independents. Some campgrounds specifically target families with children, some go for the LGBTQ crowd, some are only for those 55 and older. All have different challenges and demands of you as an owner, and all have different rewards and benefits.

Educating yourself about the various kinds of campgrounds—explained in more detail in Chapter 3—is crucial if you want to minimize the odds of getting into a bad marriage. And make no mistake: buying a campground is very much analogous to getting married, as both require a huge commitment of time and energy if they're going to last. It's no coincidence that the average time someone owns a campground before putting it up for sale is seven years, a period comparable to "the seven-year itch" popularized in a 1955 movie about marriage starring Marilyn Monroe.

A good place to start, even before buying a campground, is by paying a hundred bucks to become an associate member of the National Association of RV Parks and Campgrounds, more commonly known as ARVC. That modest investment will give you access (at an added cost) to the trade group's annual conferences and trade shows, as well as several certification programs for campground operations, but also will give you free entrée to a large on-line library of resource materials, many of which will be invaluable at this early stage of your research. Moreover, the value of the networking opportunities that membership will create for you can't be overstated, as campground owners are among the most sociable people you could hope to meet and will readily share their experiences, knowledge and resources.

(As an aside, despite its overarching name, ARVC has a byzantine membership structure that requires regular members— those who own campgrounds—-to first join an individual state association, like the Pennsylvania Campground Owners Association (PCOA) or the Virginia Campground Association (VCA). But some states, like West Virginia, don't have a state association, and other states have associations that seceded from ARVC, such as Texas and California, so in those states you ultimately will be able to join either or both the state and national organizations. None of that applies until after you own a campground, however, so for now is moot.)

Another resource worth tapping early is *Woodall's Campground Magazine*, available online or in a monthly print version with a free subscription—just be aware that as with almost every information source about the industry, Woodall's coverage is relentlessly two-dimensional, avoiding controversy and any discussion that might overshadow its subject matter. Climate change, growing campground corporatization, shoddy RV construction, extreme labor shortages—an exploration of these and many other issues critical to understanding RV parks as an industry and RVing as a social phenomenon are almost entirely absent from its pages.

So take what you can get. In this case, that includes headlines about the most recent developments affecting the industry, such as state and federal legislation, upcoming industry events, a plethora of news about industry suppliers, and rosy forecasts—disproportionately often from KOA—about the growth in camping demand and campground revenues. At least you'll get a sense of the industry's momentum and what regulatory problems it's anticipating. Of additional interest is the back-of-the-book section on Campground Investment Opportunities, which in recent years—due to changing industry dynamics—has shifted in emphasis from "campgrounds for sale" to "looking for campgrounds to buy," but which is a good starting point for identifying brokers who have campground listings.

To further broaden your education, I strongly recommend the reader-supported online publication *RVtravel*, which at times sounds almost curmudgeonly because of its unique willingness to recognize when the glass is only half-full. (Full disclosure: I have intermittently contributed articles to the site, for some of which I received a modest stipend, and *RVtravel's* founder and mainstay, Chuck Woodbury, wrote a kind intro for *Renting Dirt*.) Because it doesn't accept paid advertising, *RVtravel* can be relatively unconstrained in its coverage, and so regularly explores such topics as campground overcrowding, inadequate dealer support for RV buyers, cultural shifts among the RVing public, and safety issues such as improperly installed electrical pedestals or overweight trailers and fifth-wheels.

Since *RVtravel* is written for the RVing public in general, and not specifically for RV campground owners, a lot of its content may not seem directly relevant to you at this early stage. But if you think of campgrounds as just one segment of a complex ecosystem that includes manufacturers, suppliers, campers and RVers, as well as public campgrounds and government regulators, reading it on a regular basis will give you a better understanding of this new world you're about to enter.

There is one other educational resource to which you can turn, as long as you understand that—as with the "courses" offered by RV Park University or Heather Blankenship—there are vested interests at play that may skew their presentations. That's the "buyers' workshops" offered by several brokers, as well as by KOA and ARVC, that at their best will teach you the basics of campground valuation, balance sheet and cash-flow analysis, proper due-diligence, and the vagaries of campground financing. Such a workshop, if it's going to be useful, will typically run a couple of days—ARVC's recent efforts have been half that long—but keep in mind that the brokers who are conducting them are not doing so out of a charitable impulse: they have their own listings to promote.

That said, if you stay alert, such workshops can provide invaluable information, insights and leads. That's how Carin and I got into the business, by attending a two-day seminar led by Darrell Hess, who has since retired. Other brokers who have held such sessions include Don Dutton and the Campground Connection—listed here for informational purposes only and not as recommendations—and there may be others as well, as this is a dynamic and changing landscape.

Think about being a work-camper

Finally, there is one more thing you can do to better understand this world you're thinking about entering, and that's to become a work-camper. Somewhat like an internship in other industries, becoming a work-camper will put you on the inside of the business, giving you a first-hand look you'll never get from reading and talking with others. As a work-camper you'll see what it's like to deal with the camping public, with all its demands and expectations—and occasional rewards—but you'll also see what it takes to provide an experience you probably took pretty much for granted: the hours, the crises, the interpersonal staff dynamics.

Unlike a two-day owners' workshop, which will give you a quick aerial view of the business, work-camping requires a serious time commitment of at least six months but will get you into the trenches. It will also, with rare exception, require you to have an RV that you'll be living in for all that time—that's where the "camping" in work-camping comes in—although some very few campgrounds will have either their own RVs or other housing that they'll offer to some employees. Don't count on that, though.

Work-camping is common throughout the industry, in both private and public facilities, but can vary considerably in the details. The basic idea is that you get your RV site in exchange for your labors, up to a set amount—typically somewhere between 12 and 20 hours a week—with any additional time paid at a predetermined rate. But then there are all kinds of additional benefits that might be included. Some campgrounds may throw in free electricity, propane or wi-fi, while others may not, or may charge a discounted rate. Some will include free laundry or store discounts, and some may provide camp uniforms (usually just a shirt) while others will expect you to pay for them.

Hours and work assignments also may vary considerably. Some campgrounds will schedule one or two days off each week so you have an opportunity to explore the area, while others may require you to work a shorter day but seven days a week. Evenings and weekend work are almost a given for desk jobs, since that's when a campground has the most business coming in, but those may be the most likely times off for groundskeeping. As for the work itself, some campgrounds—especially the bigger ones—may slot you into a specific assignment so you can gain a lot of expertise; others may expose you to various assignments—housekeeping one week, weed-eating and mowing another—so they have a flexible workforce that can be shifted around as needed. This will be especially true of smaller campgrounds with a limited employee roster.

What kind of job skills do you need? Virtually anything in the construction trades is a winner, including expertise in electrical, plumbing or carpentry, as well as heavy equipment—backhoe and tractor—operations. Computer literacy and telephone skills are basic to staffing the front desk. But there also are many campground positions requiring little or no prior training, or which can be gained on the job, including housekeeping, most groundskeeping, and campground security, so a good attitude and eagerness to learn will carry you far.

If you think this is something you want to pursue, there are several ways you can approach it. One is to target campgrounds you think you'd like to experience and reach out to them directly, through mail or email and follow-up phone calls. You should start at least six months ahead of time—in the fall for a spring position, for example—and be specific about what skills you have, what positions you're willing to accept, what range of dates you're looking to work and, if you're half of a couple, whether your other half is likewise seeking a job. Many campgrounds—but not all—would rather hire a couple, because that way they can fill two jobs in exchange for giving up only one revenue-generating RV site.

Another resource for work-campers is online listings of available positions, such as *workersonwheels.com*, or recruiting workshops like those hosted by KOA, although the latter are specifically for those who want to work at a KOA. But the granddaddy of work-camping wisdom and recruitment is *Workamper News*, an online and monthly tabloid listing of campgrounds seeking work-campers, as well as listings of work-campers seeking positions. *Workamper News* also publishes a lot of tips and guidance for work-campers, offers educational webinars, manages a system for employers to rate employees—and vice versa—and, at least until the pandemic put a crimp in its operations, would host annual training workshops for newby work-campers at its Heber Springs, Arkansas headquarters.

Spending one, two or more seasons working for minimal wages before taking the next step toward campground ownership may pose a serious speedbump in your planning, and I'm not suggesting it's critical you do so. Carin and I didn't, before we took the plunge, and I'm guessing most campground owners didn't, either. On the other hand, it all comes down to how well you already understand the industry, your comfort level in dealing with ignorance or uncertainty, and whether there are any other time considerations that need to be factored in. If not, then this is one option that you might want to consider.   ♋

Chapter 3:
Narrowing the Choices

ONE THING YOU'LL QUICKLY DISCOVER about this business, if you haven't already, is how poorly defined it all is. It's not just the confusion between "campgrounds" and "RV parks" but the many different ideas about camping itself. How does it make sense to have the same word describe someone who hikes into the backcountry and sleeps in a three-pound marvel of nylon and aluminum tubing, and someone who drives a half-million-dollar motorcoach with multiple slideouts, TVs and a washer-dryer? Yet both those "campers" may end up in the same campground, and each may look down on the other, for very different reasons.

Then there's the confusion over whether a campground is primarily a residential facility or a recreational one. Are people there to live—or to live it up? The same property may host a traveling nurse who will be moving her trailer to her next job in three months, a group of Gen-Zers tenting for a weekend of campfires, beer and music, a family of six in a pop-up whose four kids want to hang out at the pool and feed the ducks, and a retired couple in a large fifth-wheel who are full-timing around the country and plan on staying with you for at least a couple of weeks. It's a mixed bag, and as the various pieces rub against each other they can produce a lot of heat.

It's therefore essential that you recognize two things as you start looking around for the campground of your dreams. The first is that no one campground can be all things to all people: that what works for one subset of the camping public will not work for another, and that trying to shoehorn a lot of conflicting expectations into a single facility will simply create a lot of headaches for you and a lot of dissatisfaction for your customers.

The second, closely related to the first, is that *you* also cannot be all things to all people. If you're to succeed you absolutely must recognize your own strengths, interests and limitations. Does a bunch of screaming kids running around set your teeth on edge? Then you definitely don't want a Jellystone franchise. Need a routine that you can pretty much count on, month after month? Maybe you should be looking more at a long-term park, in which you don't have the constant turnover—and its attendant problems—of an overnight facility. Seriously in need of a weeks- or months-long break each year? Then a seasonal park is what you're after.

To understand the universe of possibilities, let's start with definitions. RV parks are facilities expressly designed to accommodate recreational vehicles, and typically are more manicured and loaded with amenities than their plain cousins, campgrounds, which accommodate tents and may also have rental cabins. RV parks tend to be more up-scale, with some even having sites with adjoining covered patios, possibly including their own kitchens and individual bathrooms, and at the very upper end they'll call themselves RV resorts. Their amenities may include saunas, pickleball courts, water parks and restaurants.

Campgrounds, meanwhile, are more rustic and woodsy, with amenities that may include playgrounds and swimming pools, but with an overall emphasis on getting back to nature. Campgrounds, for example, are more likely to have people sitting around a campfire toasting marshmallows; RV parks might go so far as to ban individual campfires altogether (although they may have one or more centralized, "communal" firepits for the traditionalists) so that no one's RV is tainted with woodsmoke.

Even that tidy division, however, has been upended by the recent surge in "glamping," a portmanteau of "glamor" and "camping" that essentially claims you can have it all, both luxury and wilderness, or at least an illusion of the latter. Glamping most often consists of safari tents on wooden platforms, kitted out with queen or king-sized beds with high-grade linens, many including wooden partitions for bathrooms and kitchenettes; other glamping accommodations may include yurts, teepees, "covered wagons" and even treehouses, all basically presenting canvas walls as a civilized way of being in contact with nature. And while many RV parks have started incorporating glamping accommodations, there is at least one campground—operated in Maine by KOA—that has nothing but glamping tents. To add to the confusion, there are RVers, typically in the most blinged out motorcoaches, who think of themselves as glamping.

Having made that distinction, I'll note that the great majority of camping properties are neither fish nor fowl but both, usually describing themselves as "RV parks and campgrounds" and accommodating both tenters and RVers, as well as having at least a few cabins and possibly some glamping set-ups available. Throughout this book I'll be using "RV Park" and "campground" rather interchangeably, as do most people, but when you're shopping around you should be aware of the distinction.

To start, three basic questions

With that in mind, there are three initial variables you should consider in narrowing your search: for how long a season? for what kind of camper? and—perhaps most critically—where?

The seasonality issue gets to the question of how long and hard you'll be working over the course of a year. Generally speaking, campgrounds north of a frost line that's 24 inches deep—the depth to which the soil may be expected to freeze in the winter—will be open only four to six months a year, partly because few people want to go camping when it's 10 degrees outside, but mostly because it becomes much more difficult to maintain water and septic systems when you have to really bury your plumbing. In Wisconsin, for example—a state with a lot of campgrounds—the frost line can be five feet deep. That's a lot of digging at installation, and a lot more when something goes wrong.

Having a short season means everything gets compressed: you need a higher occupancy rate at higher prices in Maine than you do in Texas, just so you can get enough cash to carry you through the rest of the year. You also arguably will end up hustling a lot more to keep up with that more concentrated demand—but on the flip side, you have at least four months in which you can shut down and depart for warmer climes. (Why only four? Because you'll need a couple of months of middling weather to catch up on maintenance and to thaw everything out of its deep freeze.) As a result, a lot of campground owners in the northern tier have their own RVs, as well as standing reservations at Sun Belt campgrounds for the winter.

Perhaps surprisingly, the reverse currently does not hold true for campgrounds in the deep south or American southwest, where high humidity or triple-digit temperatures can make life miserable—but apparently not miserable enough to close RV parks. Not yet. If the summers continue getting hotter, however, it's not inconceivable that these, too, will become seasonal operations.

Turning to the question of what kind of camping customer you most want, a fundamental breakdown is between long- and short-term. Short-term campers are those who stay a week or less and include overnight travelers, tourists using your campground as a base for exploring the local area, and vacationers. Long-term campers fall into three main groups: full-timers, whose RVs are their homes; itinerant workers, such as traveling nurses or project-specific construction workers, who will move on after several months; and more-or-less local residents who leave an RV parked at your campground year-round as a summer home.

Most RV parks have some combination of the two, for reasons explored in more depth in Chapter 8. But most parks also are predominantly one or the other because of the very different kinds of campers they attract, the resulting campground climate they create, and their owners' personal preferences for what kind of facility—basically recreational, or basically residential—they want to operate.

Picking your 'campground climate'

What does "campground climate" mean? You'll get one sense of it if you drive around a campground and see unmistakable signs of permanence, such as decks and storage sheds—or in more extreme cases, attached porches, fences, elaborate landscaping or carports. The people who live in those RVs are there full time and they've taken possession of their sites, for good or ill, depending on how much pride they take in appearances and how strict the campground's rules may be. I've seen campgrounds where the long-term residents have pooled their own money and labors to create extended walkways, arbors and communal barbecue pits—and I've also seen campgrounds that look like slums or the most stereotypically Appalachian hovels, complete with discarded appliances, car parts and "No Trespassing" signs.————

Moreover, in most campgrounds dominated by full-timers, the campers' sense of ownership will extend beyond the site to the park in general. That can be a great benefit to the owner, since this possessive attitude brings extra eyes and ears to the property and deters vandalism, theft and trespassing. It also can result in a small-town atmosphere in which everyone pitches in if disaster strikes, such as cleaning up from extensive storm damage, or just for fun, as when the adults join in to put on elaborate Halloween festivities for the kids.

But just as with any small town, it also means that everyone is in everyone else's business, with all the gossip and petty rivalries that can ensue. If there are a significant number of transient sites in the campground—and especially if they're interspersed among the long-term sites, instead of being grouped together in one area—the "regulars" can create an exclusionary atmosphere that makes overnighters and short-timers feel unwelcome. And all those vested interests can create a huge problem for an owner who wants to implement major changes or rate hikes—which explains why such campgrounds often see a large exodus of full-timers shortly after new owners come aboard. In many cases, that's just as well.

While a campground with a lot of involved full-timers can leave an owner with little to do beyond regular maintenance and upkeep, a transient campground amplifies every task, from bookkeeping to traffic control to maintenance. An exponential increase in guest turnover requires higher staffing levels in the store and campground. And the increased traffic in large motorcoaches, fifth-wheels and travel trailers—many, these days, driven by campers with minimal time behind the wheel—all but ensures more physical damage to the property, as RVs are driven across lawns and backed into trees, fences, power pedestals and water hydrants.

More fundamentally, overnight and short-term guests are enormously more demanding because a lot of what they're doing is relatively new to them, and—unless they're repeat customers—everything about your campground is an unknown. They may need to be escorted to their sites, require a detailed description of your rules about campfires, quiet hours, and trash pickup, be shown how to hook up their utilities. They may need to borrow a water hose or power cable because they can't reach your hook-ups, or have maintenance bring them boards to help level their units on an uneven site. They'll want to know where they can find a good restaurant or hardware store, or how they can refill their propane tank and whether there are any local events they should plan on seeing, and all that will be thrown at you even as more RVs are rolling into the campground.

A transient campground, in other words, is a non-stop merry-go-round of demands and expectations. It requires significantly more staffing than a full-timer campground and has higher overhead expenses because of all the increased wear and tear—but because of its higher rates, it also generates significantly more revenue. And unlike a full-timer campground, which can get rather staid and settled in its ways, a transient campground is dynamic, challenging and often more rewarding for the owner because it caters to people out to have a good time. At the extremes, it's the difference between being a landlord and being a cruise ship director.

As the foregoing might suggest, whether you'll be happier

operating one kind of campground or another will depend a lot on your personal qualities and energy level. But within this basic dichotomy there are additional subcategories that you might want to research, mentioned here for reference purposes only: 55-and-over parks, which as the name suggests, are intended as kid-free zones; clothing-optional campgrounds, which while few in number draw disproportionate numbers of Canadian and European visitors; and LGBTQ+ parks, originally started as safe zones for non-binary campers but which have declined somewhat in popularity with growing social acceptance at more "mainstream" facilities.

In addition, the campground universe includes membership parks—the campground equivalent of condos—in which each site is individually owned and all the owners are assessed annual maintenance fees for upkeep of the infrastructure and common areas. It's highly unlikely that you would end up owning this kind of campground, but I've thrown it into the mix primarily to round out your overall picture of what's out there.

To be or not to be a franchisee

There is, however, one more aspect of campground ownership that you should consider, and that's whether to go with a franchise, sometimes referred to as a "business in a box" because of its standardized and packaged set of support functions.

Make no mistake: there's a lot to be gained from becoming a franchisee—especially if you're new to the business—starting with nationally recognized branding and marketing that will drive customers to your property, on to standardized software and procedures that will save you from reinventing the wheel. Both U.S. campground franchisors—yes, there are only two—will provide you with initial training, branded signage and merchandise, and annual inspections to help you recognize where you need to make improvements. They'll encourage you to attend annual conventions and trade shows, at which you'll get a chance to stay current with industry developments, as well as to network with dozens of other campground owners with an intimate understanding of the problems you face.

They're also expensive, their uniform standards can feel oppressively like micro-managing, and promises of ongoing support can be illusory. With some exceptions, you may end up feeling like you're just a cog in a large "hospitality industry" machine, which may be 180-degrees away from the reason why you wanted to own a campground in the first place.

Yogi Bear's Jellystone Park Camp-Resorts, the smaller of the two, is built around a once iconic but still persistent cartoon character who originally played a supporting role in the Huckleberry Hound Show. Few people remember Huckleberry Hound these days, but Yogi Bear lives on, his anthropomorphic character creating a strong bond even with children who have never seen one of his cartoons—and Jellystone Parks spare no effort in capitalizing on that. The result is a minor-league version of an amusement park, with arriving visitors greeted at a "Ranger Station," "Yogi Bear" making frequent appearances each day for cuddling and photo-ops, and additional appearances by his equally furry friend, BooBoo.

Add that to a supervised, activity-intensive program aimed at children 6-12, and you might rightly conclude that Jellystone Parks have an above-average payroll. But Jellystone Parks also are more capital intensive than the norm, as almost all have extensive water features—swimming pools and slides, splash parks and in some cases lazy rivers—plus such kid magnets as climbing walls, bouncing pillows, rental bikes, paddle boats, laser tag and on and on. All of which is to say, it's not cheap to become a Jellystone, even without an initial franchise fee—unlike KOA, which charges you $35,000 just to walk in the door.

As that description might suggest, Jellystones are intended as destinations—the kinds of places families visit for their entertainment value, more affordable than Disney but with more on tap than your average weekend campground. That means, among other things, that Jellystones want to appeal to all families, not just those with RVs, so while campgrounds must have a minimum of four cabins to become franchisees, most have many more. Indeed, Jellystone's parent company, Leisure Systems Inc., says cabin rentals in 2019 provided nearly a quarter of its revenues, compared with 42% of revenues from RV sites. (The balance came from store sales, activity fees and "ancillary income.") That, too, adds to the substantial capital investment that goes into a Jellystone.

KOA as the McDonald's of campgrounds

The big kid on the block, meanwhile, is KOA, which at this writing claims 540 campgrounds in its system (40 of those owned directly by the company), compared with 85 or so Jellystones. The numbers fluctuate, as new franchisees enter the system and others quit when their contracts run out, usually after five years, but the overall trend had been one of year-over-year increases. Still, it's prudent not to read too much into such numbers: at one time KOA had almost 900 franchisees, only to discover that it had absorbed too many sub-standard properties that were dragging down the whole system. Purging ensued, including an end to the KOA presence in Mexico and Japan.

Where Jellystone's marketing appeal is to families with young children, KOA's is a more generalized pitch that emphasizes consistency and minimum standards. In a marketplace still overwhelmingly dominated by one-off campgrounds ranging from the atrocious to the superlative, KOA's inherent promise is that you as a camper won't have any unpleasant surprises; it's the McDonald's of the outdoor hospitality industry, saving the camping public from greasy spoons and five-star dining alike. And, like McDonald's, it fields an impressive marketing campaign to "build trust in our brand," as one spokeswoman put it. On the other hand, just as there are people who can't stand McDonald's (or Arby's or Taco Bell), there are people who can't stand KOA, for any number of reasons.

Both franchisors require new franchisees to attend training sessions at the outset, and both have reservation platforms that tie in with QuickBooks, expediting record keeping—and providing the parent company with a ready way to levy its fees. For KOA, that's not cheap: as already mentioned, joining a KOA entails a $35,000 initial payment, plus 10% of all site fees thereafter, as well as other comparatively minor costs. Even buying a campground that's already a KOA will incur initial fees, if at a lower level.

If you decide that going with a franchise is not for you, the additional major expenses you'll have to cover will include a reservation system provider, a credit card processor and your own advertising. These days there are at least a dozen reservation systems that will be angling for your business, although the next few years should see an overall consolidation of this group, so filling this requirement is pretty much a snap for anyone who does his homework. Your choice of a reservation system will to a large extent influence whom you use for credit card processing, and should be a top subject of discussion as you shop around. Your advertising choices, meanwhile, will depend on your target audience—and, frankly, whether you need to put a whole lot of money into attracting campers at a time when soaring demand is packing 'em in.

Deciding whether you want to go the franchise route, therefore, comes down to understanding the tradeoffs and balancing those against your own needs, talents and insecurities. If an intensely kid-centric campground is not something you want to embrace, that makes it really easy to strike Jellystone from the list. Ditto if your financial resources aren't sufficient for the deeper plunge required for a Jellystone. That leaves KOA as your only franchising option, and the buy-in fee aside, it definitely has lower barriers to entry than Jellystone. On the other hand, it's become so large an operation that you stand a good chance of getting lost in the shuffle.

To end this section on a personal note, you should know— as you already do if you've read *Renting Dirt*—that the campground my family and I bought was already a KOA. We willingly but naively agreed to continue the franchise, believing that this established and widely recognized organization would provide us with the support and expertise we needed as newcomers to the industry. We were wrong. Once our five-year contract was over we bowed out, and over the next three years continued to gain business—and at a lower overhead cost.

I bring this up for two reasons. First, to underscore that few decisions are forever. If you decide to go the franchise route—and many, many KOA franchisees have had a better experience than we did—and later decide you made the wrong choice, there are exit points. On the other hand, you don't have to make this decision now—unless you end up buying an existing franchise, like we did. Assuming your campground meets certain basic requirements and isn't in an existing franchisee's non-compete area, you can always take that road once you have a better idea of the lay of the land.

The second reason is that once we left the KOA system, I was struck by how many other KOA owners contacted me to ask about our experience, and in the process revealed just how unhappy they were with their subordinate position. Again, there are many KOA franchisees for whom this is a positive relationship—but if this is something you're contemplating, it makes good business sense to talk to as many KOA owners as possible to get a fuller picture than you'll get from interacting just with the corporate sales force.

The biggest question of all: where?

Finally, there's the issue of location: generally speaking, where do you want to end up? For some, that might be a no-brainer, because of family ties or established personal preference. But for many others it's all a blank slate, with little idea of how to narrow the possibilities. Let me suggest a few considerations.

The first limiting factor, as already mentioned, is whether you're prepared to operate year-round, or only during the camping "season." You can't realistically have a campground that's open for just part of the year while everyone around you is open year-round, so if you're looking for a seasonal operation you'll automatically be relegated to the northern tier—say, above the Mason-Dixon line east of the Mississippi and more or less north of the 40th parallel through the Plains States. South of there, and all along the West Coast, you're accepting the idea that you'll be up and running year 'round.

The next—and most significant, in my view—consideration becomes meaningful only once you've understood, and accepted, that the enterprise you're contemplating is in the *outdoor* hospitality industry. I can't stress that enough. Owning and operating a campground is less like operating a hotel and much more like owning a farm, in that you're extremely vulnerable to the vagaries of weather and other environmental assaults. Barring the kind of cataclysm that results in disaster declarations, most hotels, motels and other kinds of hospitality businesses can continue operating through almost anything Mother Nature will throw at them; a campground can be shut down by just a few inches of rain or a toppled tree.

Without getting bogged down in an argument about climate change, let's agree that some parts of the country are more susceptible to certain environmental disruptions than others: earthquakes along the Pacific Coast, for example, or tornadoes in the Great Plains. And let's also agree that certain environmental assaults seem to be on the rise, for whatever reason, such as drought in the western states, or coastal flooding in the Gulf states. The question you therefore should answer is how comfortable you are with each of these threats—keeping in mind that there is no such thing as a threat-free paradise—and how that comfort level might change if things get worse.

My wife, for example, was raised in northern Illinois and as a result has a visceral fear of tornadoes that made the idea of buying a campground in the Great Plains not even subject to negotiation. On the other hand, there are many campgrounds in tornado alley that have built underground storm shelters and have used them as a marketing strategy, pitching their shelters to campers and RVers—and there will always be campers and RVers, even in tornado country, even if they're just passing through—as a way of distinguishing themselves from competitors.

On the other hand, both of us lived in Arizona for many years, and so have paid special attention to a drought that has only intensified over the past decade. It remains inconceivable to us that Phoenix remains one of the fastest growing cities in the country, even as that state was hit in 2021 with reduced water allocations from the Central Arizona Project for the first time in its history—and with more such cuts inevitably on the way. Unlike tornadoes, which while potentially devastating are hit-and-miss, are of short duration and can be defended against, there's really nothing you can do to provide water that isn't there. It shouldn't be necessary to point out that RVers have wheels that can take them elsewhere when things get grim; campgrounds don't have that mobility, which is why we wouldn't even consider buying one in a persistently drought-afflicted area.

Think like a farmer, not a hotelier

When balancing environmental threats, therefore, it makes more sense to evaluate them the way a farmer might, rather than as a hotelier. If choosing between farming/campground operating in Nevada or Arizona vs. Tennessee or Missouri, for example, your long-term prospects might be better in the latter—even if your crops get wiped out this year by a freak storm, you can probably replant next season. But as the Hohokam and other ancient civilizations in the American southwest attest, there are some disasters from which there is no rapid recovery.

Other environmental concerns are less clear-cut, but still need to be weighed. The earthquakes that menace the Pacific Coast states are, like tornadoes, relatively rare even as they can be highly destructive. But the wildfires that increasingly are devastating all the states west of the Great Plains are both more frequent and more widespread with each passing year, not only consuming millions of acres of prime camping and outdoor recreation areas, but filling the air with noxious smoke over millions of acres more.

And while rebuilding from an earthquake is painful and expensive, it's still less problematic than trying to restore a piece of scorched earth as a vacation paradise.

For an industry that touts itself as a way of reconnecting with nature, however, campgrounds and RV parks spend remarkably little attention to environmental concerns. Both state and national trade groups are absent from public discussions about social responses to climate change, emerging from the woodwork only when there's a possibility legislation might be enacted that would crimp their style. When California recently pondered an environmental rule change to ban small gasoline engines—like those used in many RV generators—for instance, industry response focused on how that would inconvenience RVers instead of how it would help clear the air those RVers (and everyone else) are breathing.

That myopic outlook characterizes even the biggest industry participants, who otherwise might be expected to have the expertise and deep pockets to make course corrections that smaller operators just can't afford. So, for example, despite the growing incidence and severity of hurricanes in the Gulf and along the south Atlantic coast, KOA spent millions to rebuild its RV park in the Florida Keys, and millions more to rebuild on North Carolina's Outer Banks. If they can dodge a bullet for five or six years they may recoup that investment, but that kind of profligate tenacity will be out of your reach—and if they bet wrong, they have the capacity to absorb a loss that you can't because they're so well diversified across the country.

What all that means for you is that you won't encounter much—if any—discussion of environmental challenges when you're looking at various properties, or if you attend seminars about campground risk factors. It's going to be up to you to educate yourself, and to pose the relevant questions to brokers and sellers. They're not going to volunteer such information, and often it won't even be because they're trying to hide anything. It's just not the way they think.

Where to start? One place, unsurprisingly, is with Google

maps, where you can find maps plotting just about any variable that might concern you. When we were doing our research, we found one especially useful map that overlaid areas of high earthquake, tornado and hurricane activity—information that played a significant role in us ending up in the Shenandoah Valley. Your results might differ. You also might want to map numerous other variables, such as drought, forest fires, flooding and seawater rise. You might want to chart areas of high bark-beetle or other destructive insect infestation, or map the extent of surface mining or fracking.

The point, again, is not so much to find the non-existent perfect spot, but to narrow your search to those areas where you think your investment has the best survival chances. ❧

Finding and buying what you want

Chapter 4:
Starting the Search

ONCE YOU'VE GOTTEN PAST the preliminary steps outlined in Chapters 2 and 3, you'll have enough guidelines to keep you focused in your search for an acceptable campground. You'll know, more or less, what kind of park you want to buy. You'll know, more or less, where you're willing to go—or, perhaps more critically, where you don't want to go. But how do you start?

The first and most obvious jumping off point is the internet, where a search for "campgrounds for sale" will produce half-a-dozen listings of brokers on the first search page, including Campground Connections, Campground Marketplace, and Parks and Places. Most will list their inventory, sorted geographically and by price and including thumbnail descriptions and photos, but you'll soon find that the quality and amount of information may vary enormously. In many cases, you may not find the name of the campground that's for sale, or even precisely where it's located.

Moreover, some brokers may not show *any* properties for sale, enticing you to contact them by displaying what they've sold, rather than what's available: that's what Darrell Hess, who managed to grab the *campgroundsforsale.com* URL many years ago and who more recently has slipped into semi-retirement, has been doing. Hess maintains what the industry calls "pocket listings," or leads on campgrounds that their owners may be willing to sell at the right price but which they're not actively marketing. That secretiveness may be frustrating to you as a potential buyer, but from the broker's point of view it winnows out the idle window-shoppers. From your perspective, there's nothing to lose by firing off a query about what may be available, even if a broker's site doesn't show any "for sale" listings.

You'll also find sites like *rvparkstore.com*, which is associated with RVPark University (discussed briefly in Chapter 2) and which amounts to a poorly administered bulletin board. Accessible to brokers and individual campground owners alike, its listings often include property with only tenuous campground connections, including marinas (without RV sites) or vacant land (which could possibly be developed into a campground). For all the dross you'll have to pick through to find anything of value, this site nevertheless is worth a look on the off chance you'll find a property listed by someone who's trying to avoid paying a 3% to 7% broker's fee. Just learn to be patient.

Finally, both KOA and Jellystone have online-listings of franchised campgrounds for sale, if that's the direction you want to take. Be aware, however, that these lists are not exhaustive— franchised parks for sale may list with outside brokers instead of with the franchisor. The Jellystone site, meanwhile, includes a few useful tips of what you should look for if you want to buy a campground for subsequent conversion to the Jellystone system.

There are alternatives to working with brokers, and reasons I'll explore later for being wary of them, but those methods will require a lot more work from you and ultimately may be unproductive. I mention them here mostly as a supplement to the broker route, rather than as a substitute, as there's no reason why you shouldn't conduct your search as broadly as possible. And while sellers are contractually bound to a single broker, you as a buyer are not and can—and should—work with whoever can deliver what you need.

The most obvious first step is to start networking with state campground associations, as well as chambers of commerce and realtors in the areas that interest you. Let them know you're in the market. Ask if they know of any campground owners who have been thinking about selling but haven't taken that first step. A little bit of schmoozing and liberal dispensation of a business card can go a long way toward tapping information reservoirs you didn't know existed—and the contacts you make now will help you when you actually own a local business.

A more direct approach is simply to start cold-calling in an area in which you're interested. Compile a list of possible candidates from the Good Sam Campground Directory, which has the most comprehensive state-by-state listings and a thumbnail description of each campground and RV park, sorted by municipality, and start sending out letters or emails asking if the owner has any interest in selling. A surprising number will, but don't get too excited—a lot of people take the attitude that anything is for sale at the "right" price, which you'll find is right for them but completely out of the question for anyone else. Nevertheless, you'll ignite enough flickers of interest to make this a worthwhile approach.

What to expect from brokers

Whether or not these efforts pan out, however, you'll still be looking at brokers' listings and at some point will be dealing with one or more of them. Your initial point of contact probably will occur because of a listing that has piqued your interest and about which you want more information. Be prepared to answer a few basic questions, including roughly how much you're prepared to pony up for a down payment, but the heavy lifting will come later; right now, you'll be asked to sign a non-disclosure agreement in which you agree not to share any information you receive. You should do so if you want to learn more.

In addition to the non-disclosure agreement, you may expect multiple warnings that stress the confidentiality of the entire situation. While you might think that campground owners would want the world to know their property is for sale—how else will they attract buyers?—in fact, many try to keep that decision a secret from their customers and their employees, for fear that the news will drive them away. Change can be destabilizing, so there may be some basis to that anxiety, but the truth also is that brokers actively encourage a *sub rosa* approach for fear of losing the sale—and therefore their commission—to someone else. That's why, for example, so many listings are non-specific about a campground's location, as a deterrent to potential buyers from doing an end-run and contacting the owner directly.

What you should expect in return for signing the nondisclosure form is a more complete description of the campground and of the surrounding area, as well as three years of basic financial information. The description, usually including photos, should be comprehensive enough for you to visualize the property and its capacity, as well as what makes this park attractive to campers; the financials should give you enough information to make an initial assessment of whether the campground is being fairly priced. So, for example, some of the basics you should be able to learn at this preliminary stage include:

• The campground acreage, together with a general description of the terrain. Is it heavily wooded? Flat or rolling? Any water features, such as a stream or pond?

• The number of RV sites, broken down by type (pull-throughs and back-ins) and utilities (how many full hook-ups, how many water and electric, as well as how many 30 amp and how many 50 amp?). Comparing the number of sites with the total acreage will be a particularly helpful metric: anything more than eight sites per acre suggests little if any room for internal expansion or added amenities—and, indeed, may be on the claustrophobic side.

• How many improved tent sites (something more than a patch of grass) and how many cabins? How many can the cabins sleep, and how old are they?

• The number and size of various infrastructure buildings, such as a camp store/registration area, bathhouses, maintenance sheds, game rooms and pavilions. How old are they, and how serviceable?

• Whether the campground is on a municipal well and sewer system, or on a well and/or septic system. If the campground has its own sewage treatment plant, that should lead to a slew of questions about licensing, operator training and effluent testing.

• What other amenities does the park have, such as a swimming pool, playgrounds, horseshoe pits, bouncing pillows or climbing equipment?

• Is there owner housing, or housing for employees?

The information you want about the surrounding area gets to the question of why people come to this campground in the first place, or how it might be marketed in the future. How far are you from major metro areas that can drive customers to your property? Are you near an interstate, in which case you can expect a preponderance of overnighters; or do campers have to drive off the beaten path to reach you, in which case you'll be targeting longer stays? What natural attractions are in the area, such as lakes or hiking and biking trails, or what tourist attractions, such as museums, shopping outlets or historical sites? Lacking one or both, does the campground provide enough amenities to be its own destination, rather than serve largely as a base camp for other excursions?

Financial information is key

But it's the financial information that will be key to whether you'll take a closer look at any particular listing. No matter how many bells and whistles it has, no matter how beautiful the property or how impressive its amenities, all of that is simply flesh draped over an underlying financial skeleton that has to be sturdy enough to carry it, plus whatever it's going to cost you to buy and operate the place. And if the financial superstructure is not sturdy enough today, you must have a clear vision of how you're going to make it that way—and pockets sufficiently deep enough to carry you that far.

Although you'll do a deeper dive into the numbers once you're closer to making an offer, what you want to know for your initial screening is how much a property has been taking in each year, and what it's been costing to run the business. The revenues are relatively easy to identify, with site registration fees comprising the lion's share, followed by store sales and special fees. Depending on how the cash flow statement is structured, propane sales, firewood and ice may be their own line items or may be rolled in with the rest of the store sales, but if you don't see them listed, ask. Special fees may include cancellation fees, site lock fees or pet fees, and if the campground has a heavy activity schedule or a lot of amenities, also may include activities fees. There also may be a line item for metered electric charges, although these usually are pass-through payments from long-term campers to the utility company and not actual income; in most jurisdictions, campgrounds are not permitted to make a profit from electricity resales.

The income categories just described should then be adjusted by subtracting the cost of goods—what the campground paid for the store stock, propane, firewood and ice that it resold—to come up with a gross profit. You'll then balance that against the campground's operating expenses: that is, everything it costs to run the business on a regular basis, including advertising, licenses and permits, credit card fees, payroll, liability insurance, maintenance parts and supplies, utilities, taxes and so on. Operating expenses do *not* include mortgage or loan interest or payments to the owner, since those will vary from one owner to another.

The difference between gross profit and adjusted operating expenses will be the campground's net operating income, the single most crucial number you'll want to know. Net operating income, commonly abbreviated NOI, tells you how much you can reasonably expect—all other things being equal—to take in each year to cover your own mortgage payments and personal profit. It's the number your banker will want to know to determine if you'll be able to service your debt. And it's the number you'll want to contrast with the campground's asking price, to determine if the seller is asking too much.

Here's an example to make that clear: let's say Campground X pulled in $500,000 last year in gross profit (all revenues minus cost of goods) and had $450,000 in expenses, which included $100,000 in mortgage payments and a $50,000 draw that the campground owner paid to himself. Subtracting the expenses from the gross leaves you with $50,000; adding back the $100,000 in mortgage payments and the $50,000 draw yields $200,000 in adjusted net operating income, which is the amount you can reasonably infer will be available for you to cover your own interest payments and money to live on. Is that going to be enough?

Calculating and using capitalization rates

The answer depends on several variables, which I'll explore in more depth in Chapter 5. But for your purposes right now, as a screening tool, what you want to look at is the campground's asking price. Take the net operating income you just calculated, $200,000, and divide that by the asking price to get what's called a capitalization rate—your potential rate of return on your investment. If the asking price is $2,000,000, your cap rate in this example is 10%; if the asking price is $3,000,000, the cap rate is 6.6%. Generally speaking, a higher cap rate indicates a riskier investment, and vice versa. The cap rate for most campground sales should be somewhere between 8% and 12%, although it's been known to go as low as 5% and as high as 15%.

(Cap rates are widely used in commercial real estate investing of all sorts, and if this is your primary reason for buying a campground, there are numerous readily accessible resources to better describe how they're best used. However, because campgrounds—like bed-and-breakfasts—usually are a hybrid of commercial and residential investing, their usefulness is somewhat diluted and cap rates should be treated more as guidelines than as hard-and-fast decision points.)

If that sounds too complicated this early in your search, here's a quick-and-dirty way to approach the numbers: the asking price should be between three and four times the gross profit. Sticking with the same example, that means a $2,000,000 asking price would be four times the $500,000 gross profit—equivalent to the 10% cap rate we just calculated. A $1.5 million asking price (three times gross) would be equal to a 13.3% cap rate—which, if you can find it, deserves a serious look—whereas a $3 million asking price would be six times the gross profit, suggesting this is one deal you should either renegotiate or walk away from.

If cap rates have been known to go as low as 5%, what's wrong with 6.6%? Why not pay six- or seven-times gross profit? There are at least two reasons, starting with the understanding that cap rates are indicators of risk levels. Just as treasury bonds pay lower interest rates—in essence, have a lower cap rate—than junk bonds because they're backed by the full faith and credit of the United States, campgrounds with extremely low cap rates are presenting themselves as low-risk investments. In the real world, however, the opposite is more likely. One bad storm can throw all those optimistic expectations into the crapper, and especially so if you want to operate a northern tier park with a four-month season.

The other reason you should walk away from extraordinarily low cap rates is because of what they mean for your debt service coverage ratio. Unless you're prepared to put down substantially more than the 25%-30% expected by your lender, a low cap rate means you won't have a sufficient NOI cushion to assure a bank you won't default and it won't want to bankroll your purchase.

That said, a lot of those rules go out the window if you're a large player with very deep pockets who has the wherewithal to make capital investments the previous owners couldn't afford, but which will yield outsized returns to the bottom line. Presumably that's what motivated Sun Outdoors to spend $17 million in 2021 for a Virginia campground that had sold just one year earlier for $3 million. You might be able to do something similar, if on a much smaller scale, if you see a campground with a lot of unrealized potential that you have the money and energy to develop, but understand that this is a speculative approach that takes a lot of savvy and high risk tolerance.

Why prices get distorted

All of the foregoing exlains why you need to look at list prices analytically, but it doesn't explain why those prices can be so out of whack with financial reality. You might think sellers would price their properties more realistically, since their ultimate goal is to find a buyer, but that doesn't take into account two dynamics that are distorting the market.

The first, which has always been true, is the same reason cap rates have less applicability to RV parks as compared to, say, a self-storage warehouse: most family-owned campgrounds are both a business and a home. The latter introduces an emotional component that selling most businesses won't have, since a huge amount of the seller's identity and personal history is usually wrapped up in the property. You may, in fact, encounter a significant ambivalence that becomes even stronger as the possibility of a sale increases—to such an extent that the seller will start throwing up new conditions or requirements that unconsciously sabotage a transaction.

An indefensibly high asking price can be a sign of such ambivalence, but it also can be indicative of a seller's misplaced judgment of values. Just as someone selling a home may think their bathroom upgrades justify a higher price than a potential buyer finds agreeable, a campground owner may be thinking that all the money he sank over the past couple of years into cabins or major amenities should be coming back to him as part of the purchase price—if he hadn't made those capital investments, after all, he might be sitting on that cash today. Unfortunately, that seller is going to be disappointed, since the return on those capital investments will come only over several years, in the form of increased business or higher rates, and not as a sales price add-on.

The other dynamic distorting the marketplace is the pandemic-induced buying frenzy described in Chapter 1, with so much institutional money flowing into the "outdoor hospitality" sector that greed has prevailed over prudence. Early in 2021, for example, a Michigan based campground broker's listings featured a slew of jaw-dropping asking prices, from a nine-acre seasonal camp-ground in Alaska with gross sales of $23,315, priced at $385,000, to a 17.5-acre property in the Midwest with gross sales of just under $300,000, priced at $2.5 million. Meanwhile, a KOA Journey with 62 sites, 6 cabins and $178,156 in gross revenues was up for grabs at a smidge below $2 million.

If you're paying attention, you'll note that these asking prices run up to 16 times gross revenues. You might want to buy a home in Alaska for $385,000, which given current home prices is not an outlandish amount, and make a little money on the side by renting to some RVers—just don't kid yourself into thinking you'll have a viable business. In the B&B realm this would be known as a "lifestyle" property, that is, a property that doesn't have enough guest rooms to carry the business—the renting out of rooms is intended primarily to help defray your home mortgage.

Time to hit the road

Once you've screened your initial candidates and identified campgrounds that meet your basic criteria and are fairly priced, you're ready to put boots on the ground: road trip! This can be fun, but it's also expensive and can take a lot of time. Keep good records of your expenses for tax purposes, including odometer readings for mileage claims.

One thing you'll quickly learn as you make your visits is that the reality rarely matches the photos you've been sent and the mental pictures you've created. With some exceptions, the camp-grounds will look smaller and scruffier than you'd envisioned, the owners either more brusque or more weary than you'd expected. If you're running around in winter, the campgrounds will look bleak and muddy; if it's the summer, you'll be tripping over people and the grounds may look surprisingly overgrown. Take it all in stride, trying to look beneath surface appearances to grasp the basics.

If you're working through a broker, you may discover you're not as free as you wish to poke your nose into everything, or to have a frank discussion with the seller. One hurdle is the effort by most brokers to keep a potential sale a secret for as long as possible, which means your presence must somehow be explained away. This is less of a problem up north if it's December or January and campers and employees are in short supply, but at other times and places you'll be lying through your teeth or being uncomfortably evasive, claiming you're inspecting the property for a wedding party or an RV club outing, or pretending to be an insurance agent appraising the property for a new policy, or whatever else you might concoct.

You also may find that your broker will insist on "showing" you the property, instead of letting you meet the owner and taking an initial look on your own. By being relentlessly present in any conversation you have with the seller, the broker may inhibit candid answers to your questions—or worse, may end up answering questions that you'd prefer were answered by the owner. Enough of this and you'll eventually understand that "your" broker is not yours at all: that a broker's basic goal is to sell you a campground, and in pursuit of that goal, many will attempt to put everything in the best possible light. To the extent most campground owners—given the chance—will be at least somewhat frank in discussing problem areas in their operation, the broker who insists on shepherding you will limit that kind of interaction as much as possible.

Not all brokers are that intrusive, of course, so if that describes the one you're working with, think seriously about finding someone else. Your purpose at this point is to identify your top candidates for acquisition, and the more unfiltered information you can gather, the more thorough your vetting will be. Your broker should be enabling that process, not getting in the way of it.

As you look around, question anything you see, especially if it differs from the information you've already been given. Look for possible maintenance issues that you'll want to examine more closely if talks get serious: signs of water damage in public buildings? Peeling paint or visibly rotting wood on door frames? Gravel roads that appear prone to rutting or potholes? Assess whether all sites have both a picnic table and (usually) a fire ring, and evaluate how level they are. Ask about the age of the pool and when it was last refinished, how many septic tanks there are and how often they get pumped out, how much snow might be expected in any one season and what capacity the campground has to clear its roads. Look at the maintenance area and the large equipment— mowers, tractors, skid-steers, trucks, etc.—that may be there and ask if any of it is leased. Find out how the campground obtains its firewood for resale.

Don't get bogged down in the weeds, but do see enough and ask enough to have any big problem areas jump out at you so you can determine if there's a good enough fit for you to take a much deeper look. Few campgrounds will check all your boxes, so if what you see is acceptable except for a couple of things, think about—and perhaps ask the existing owner for his or her thoughts—on how you might correct or compensate for the inevitable shortcomings. If, for example, you're looking for a campground you can operate with your grown son and his family but there's only one owner residence, what can you do to make up the shortfall? Is there room for another double-wide? Or nearby housing for sale? Whatever you find, you'll want to factor that into your mental calculations about how much you'll be spending.

Understand also that unless you and a seller agree other-wise, you'll be buying the campground "as is." That doesn't mean you can't negotiate a lower price or make other adjustments to compensate for an expensive problem, but if you see a lot of red flags at this stage you might want to move on. Otherwise, assuming that what you've found is mostly acceptable, you'll be ready to move on to making an offer. ⁀૩

Chapter 5:
Making an Offer

YOU'VE SPENT MONTHS NARROWING your search for the campground you want to buy, and after some false starts you think you've found the one. It's the right size, in the right area, with an asking price that's within your range, and you've spent enough time chatting with the owner to feel comfortable about making an offer. If you haven't already done so, now would be a good time to get a good real estate attorney, as well as a certified public accountant.

One of the first decisions you'll need to make is: who is buying the campground? You almost certainly don't want to buy it in your name, because that puts you on the hook for any liability that might arise. Most small businesses are owned either by a limited liability company or an S corporation, either of which will provide some protection for your personal assets if there are claims against the campground or if it fails as a business, but the differences between the two and the different tax consequences of each make this a subject for you to discuss with your CPA or lawyer.

There also are other ownership possibilities, depending on how you're going to finance the acquisition. The most notable example is if you plan on using the untaxed assets of an IRA or 401(k) pension plan through a process called Rollovers for Business Startups, which despite the unfortunate ROBS acronym, is a Congressionally authorized way to create a business funding vehicle via retirement assets. The process is tightly regulated and typically administered by an established ROBS provider, like Benetrends or Guidant, and in all cases requires your registration as a class C corporation. This, too, is something you will want to discuss with your white-collar professionals. If you go this route, make sure you also ask them about its implications for your exit strategy.

One other thing you might want to determine at the out-set is whether you want to acquire the campground in one or two pieces—as a package deal, or as simultaneous purchases of the land and of the business as a separate piece. In this kind of ownership structure, Limited Liability Company A buys the land, Limited Liability Company B (both these entities with you as the man-aging partner) buys the business, and LLC A then rents the land to LLC B. Although this simply looks like shifting money from one pocket to the other, both in the same pair of pants, it's simply another way to shield some of your assets if there's a liability claim against the campground. Again, this is something you should dis-cuss with your CPA and attorney.

Finally, as you move toward making an offer, you'll need to know how you're going to pay for your acquisition. Unless you're lucky enough be sitting on a sufficient pile of cash or liquid assets, or have family and friends who are bankrolling you, you'll have to get financing, which typically comes from a commercial bank. But another source of funding that's perhaps more common in the campground industry than in other lines of business is from the seller himself—and that's a possibility you should raise if he doesn't. He won't be surprised if you do.

Some sellers, obviously, just want to get their money and be done with it. Others, however, may not want all that income in one taxable lump sum and would prefer to spread out payments over several years, earning interest along the way. From your per-spective, meanwhile, having some (or even all) of the sales price covered by seller-financing means you can apply for a smaller bank loan, which may make a banker more receptive to your applica-tion. This was a bigger consideration prior to the pandemic, when campgrounds were more of a niche investment product than they are today and many loan officers were nervous about lending into an industry they didn't understand, but a fair amount of uncer-tainty persists nonetheless. Having the seller keep a hand in the game, with its implicit endorsement of you as the buyer, can be reassuring to a banker.

Of course, all financial arrangements involve risks, and because seller financing plays second fiddle to any bank loans, sellers are more vulnerable in case of a default. The last thing a seller wants is to repossess the property he just sold because you're not keeping up your payments, so even though you may not jump through as many hoops to earn a seller's confidence as you would a banker's, you nonetheless will have to earn his trust, through your demeanor, your credit rating and history, and any additional assurances that will be woven into your final purchase agreement. Moreover, if you do get seller financing, don't be surprised if there's some nervous hovering until the seller is assured you've got everything under control.

Taking the plunge

Once the above variables are nailed down, you're prepared to make an offer. This can be pretty scary, because you might feel you really don't know enough to be sure you're not over-paying. Most of the information you've received is coming from the seller, and you don't know if it's complete or if it's accurate. You're about to shovel an enormous percentage of your net worth—quite possibly all of it—into what might be a money-pit, and there's no way of knowing at this point if you're about to make the worst mistake of your life. And you'll be putting down a deposit of $10,000 to $20,000 or more to demonstrate good faith, which feels like a substantial commitment.

Relax.

Although making an offer sounds final, it's really just the initial step in a process with at least a couple of off-ramps, should you decide to bail. The first is that any offer will be contingent on your review of the property, including Phase I environmental testing, confirmation of the title and your evaluation of all on-site utilities, infrastructure and improvements—in other words, even though you've agreed to buy the campground, that agreement isn't final until you've had the opportunity to kick the tires and look under the hood. That inspection will be accommodated during a due diligence period, as defined in a purchase contract, and essentially will give you the right to walk away without penalty if for any reason you're dissatisfied with what you find.

A second off-ramp will be provided in the purchase contract if your purchase is contingent on obtaining outside financing—as most such transactions are. If you make a good-faith effort to get a necessary bank loan but are turned down, that also is sufficient reason to rescind the agreement without penalty. (For the main elements of a sale and purchase agreement, including the inspection period and contingencies, see Appendix C)

If you're dealing directly with the seller—without a broker in the middle—your first step will be to draft an offer letter that identifies the property in question; your proposed purchase price, as well as any seller financing you may require; your needed inspection period and proposed closing date; your list of contingencies; and a binding statement of exclusivity, which simply means the campground owner will not be dealing with other potential buyers while your efforts proceed. This is not the final agreement—indeed, whereas the offer letter may be little more than a single page, the final agreement typically will run to 10 or 15 pages—but by signing it, both parties agree to its main points and to make a good faith effort to negotiate a definitive agreement within a specific time, such as 30 days.

Understand that the offer letter is merely an opening salvo, based on your needs and on whatever prior communication you've had with the seller that leads you to believe he'll agree. But until it's signed by both parties, everything is up for grabs, so if the offer contains elements that have been discussed only sketchily, or not at all, this will be the time to nail them down. That means agreeing on the purchase price. It means that if the seller has consented to carry a note so you don't have to line up as much bank financing, that you've agreed on the amount and its terms. And it means agreeing on the overall schedule and on the contingencies under which you might pull out. Trying to change any of these points after the offer letter has been signed will end badly, so make sure you're at peace with what you're presenting. (See Appendix A for a sample of what an offer letter might look like.)

If you're working through a broker, the offer letter won't be necessary—the broker will gladly work with both parties to craft a comprehensive purchase and sale agreement that both buyer and seller find acceptable before getting signatures. This will include not only the provisions that go into an offer letter, but all the other details that you'd otherwise be negotiating on your own after an offer letter is signed. Among other things, this will include:

• The purchase price, the amount of down payment (the money you'll be personally putting down), and the amount of your deposit, which may be forfeited if you don't meet the negotiated schedule.

• The amount of bank financing you'll require and the date by which it must be obtained. Failure to obtain such financing after a good-faith effort will void the contract but will return the deposit.

• The terms of seller financing, if any. This is the amount the seller agrees to carry, sometimes for tax reasons, and becomes a second mortgage, behind the bank financing.

• A schedule for the seller to provide copies of various documents, including the existing title policy, service and supply contracts, licenses and permits, any environmental and engineering reports and financial operating statements for the previous three years.

• A deadline for acceptance of the contract, a specified due diligence period—typically 60 to 90 days—and a closing date, between a week and two weeks after your inspection is completed.

• A legal description of the property, as well as a list of all equipment and fixtures that will convey.

There is much more, of course, having to do with prorating taxes, assessments, and site reservations and payments, but most of that is pretty formulaic. There may also be more specific provisions, for example, if you're buying an existing franchised park, or if you're required to provide a personal guarantee for seller financing. But once the contract is signed, on presentation by a broker or within 30 days after an offer letter has been accepted, the heavy lifting begins. This is known as the due diligence period, and it's going to be your best effort to learn as much as you can about your pending purchase so there are as few nasty surprises as possible. Depending on the age of the campground and how thorough you want to be, it also can get pretty pricey. Peace of mind, alas, is not cheap.

Keep in mind that the campground is being sold "as is." Keep in mind also that anything with as many moving parts as an RV park is going to have some blemishes—or worse—and the longer the owner has been in a "seller" frame of mind, the greater the odds that you'll be encountering deferred maintenance as well. You're not looking for perfection. You are looking for problems that will have to be addressed, and you'll have to decide for yourself whether they're ones you can accept, whether you're going to require the seller to correct them prior to a sale, or whether they're enough to justify renegotiating the sales price or other contract terms. If the answer to the first two is "no" and you can't get the seller to budge on the sales price, the smart money says you should walk away.

Figure out the revenues and expenses

On the business end of things, you'll want to take a close look at three years of profit and loss statements to see where money has come from and where it's been going. What are the site rates, when were they last adjusted and how do they compare to the campground's nearest competitors? Is there an online booking system, and does it include dynamic pricing (in which rates vary in response to supply and demand) or are prices largely static, varying perhaps only by time of year or on weekdays vs. weekends? Are there other fees associated with booking, such as cancellation penalties or lock fees (a surcharge for guaranteeing a specified site)? What are the occupancy rates on weekends? Mid-week?

What other sources of income are there? If there is a campground store, what percentage of overall revenues does it contribute (ideally 10% or more, but considerably less if there's a supermarket within a few miles)? Does the campground sell alcohol? If not, is that an overlooked income source, or are there other limiting factors? Does it sell firewood, propane or ice, and if so, what is the markup on those items and who are the suppliers? Are there activities fees, and if so, how much and for what? Golf car, paddle boat or bicycle rentals? Keep poking at the numbers until you get a fairly clear idea of where the money is coming from and can start thinking about what revenue sources might be enhanced or how the cost of goods can be reduced.

On the other side of the ledger, how has the campground been spending money? Look especially closely at two things: payroll and maintenance. Payroll at most campgrounds historically ran between 25% and 30% of operating costs, but the pandemic and its associated "great resignation" have thrown that calculation for a loop, with the minimum wage no longer sufficient to keep workers—and workers harder to find even at higher pay. Try to get a handle on headcount vs. payroll numbers, and don't be surprised if payroll is at 35% of costs or higher. Keep in mind also that payroll totals may be affected by the number of work-campers, and suss out whether those totals include payments to the owner—and if so, how much that has been.

Maintenance—of grounds, buildings and equipment, which may be broken out separately or lumped together—is another line item that may vary considerably, depending on which items have been expensed (which means they'll be entered in the P&L) and which have been booked as capital improvements (putting them on the balance sheet). Does ten tons of gravel for the roads count as an operating expense, because it needs repeating every so many months? Or is it a capital improvement, because it exceeds an arbitrary dollar amount? An argument can be made either way, but depending on your campground's bookkeeping choices, maintenance costs may be either significantly higher or lower than they would be if someone else were keeping the books.

Other major expenses you'll want to look at—and ask about, as necessary—include advertising and marketing, which arguably can be reined in at a time of unprecedented demand; campground insurance, which too many campground owners skimp on; and utilities, with electricity inevitably the biggest cost but not entirely beyond your ability to moderate. If the RV park has long-term campers, for instance, but doesn't meter and charge for the electricity they use, it's a sure bet that usage on those sites will decrease dramatically once those campers have to pay for what they use. Indeed, it wouldn't hurt to have meters on all the bigger sites, even for over-nighters, against the day when charging big rigs or electric vehicles will become the norm.

Other things you'll want to look at

Legal considerations you'll want to check on include zoning, and if the campground is operating with a variance or special use permit, whether that variance or SUP will transfer automatically to a new owner or whether you'll need to make an application. Similarly, make sure to ask about any aspect of the campground that has been "grandfathered in," usually because a rule or regulation enacted after the campground was operating would make it non-compliant: will the grandfathered exception apply to a new owner, as well? Are there changes or improvements you might want to make that could nullify a grandfathered exemption, such as expanding a building that hasn't been compliant with setback restrictions?

You'll need a title search for a bank loan, but also might want to invest in a survey to firmly establish property boundaries and any easements that might come with them. If the campground is on a well and its own septic system, you'll want to visit with the health department to determine what permits, if any, you might need to operate a waterworks and what limits there may be on the number of allowed septic connections. If the campground has a swimming pool or if it sells propane, you should determine if you need particular training or certification to operate one or both. If the campground sells prepared food that's another set of permitting regulations you'll have to investigate, and ditto if it operates its own sewage treatment system.

Your purchase contract should include a provision for a Phase 1 Environmental Site assessment, which will be required by any commercial lender to ensure it isn't underwriting a liability nightmare. The assessment, for which you'll need to retain an environmental consulting firm, will determine if your target property has or is likely to have (as in the case of oil or gas exploration on an adjacent parcel) environmental contamination. The contract also should address whether there are underground storage tanks or high radon readings in campground buildings, both fairly standard provisions for most real estate purchases. You also should inquire about floodplain maps, hazardous waste audits and any endangered or protected species reports affecting the property. And you should learn if there are any pending legal actions against the property and if they will be resolved before closing.

Because you'll be operating a facility open to the public, you'll also need to wade into the complexities of the Americans with Disabilities Act of 1990, including two provisions that are especially relevant to campgrounds. The first is a requirement that non-zero-entry swimming pools (those with steps) have a chair lift enabling disabled campers to access the amenity—which many campgrounds still don't have, even though the compliance deadline was 2013. The second is that the campground's website must be handicapped-compliant, which has to do with how the site manages text and graphics for the benefit of the visually impaired. Although this aspect of the ADA applies to all businesses, a cottage industry of predatory attorneys has specifically targeted RV parks—especially in the northeast—on behalf of clients who in many cases haven't even been to the campground.

You'll need a physical assessment, too

Bewildering enough as that may seem, all the foregoing touches only on the operation's business aspects. Still awaiting you is an examination of the physical property itself, a job which becomes trickier the longer the campground has been around. A first step is to take the list of equipment and fixtures that was provided with the purchase contract and match it against the reality. If the list says there are six golf cars, two tractors, a dump truck and three trailers, check to see that the actual numbers agree—and while you're at it, see what kind of shape they're in. Are there maintenance logs you can inspect, or service records?

Walk the property and confirm the number and types of cabins or park models, as well as the number and types of RV sites: how many back-ins, how many pull-throughs, how many full-hookups, how many with 50 amps, and so on. Take a tape measure and verify site sizes, making sure they're at least 25 feet wide—and ideally more than 30. Are the RV pads gravel, or are they concrete or asphalt? Do an inventory of fire rings—if the campground provides those—and picnic tables, ensuring there's one at each site, including any tent sites. If there are water features, such as a lake or streams, look for signs of past flooding and ask what you should expect in case of extreme rainfall. Look overhead at any foliage to assess the general health of the tree canopy, and ask if there's a regular tree maintenance program whose records you can inspect.

You'll also want to get an understanding of the basic infrastructure—the water, electric, sewer and wi-fi systems—much of which will be underground and relatively inaccessible. This will be especially problematic in an older campground, but even newer campgrounds may have cut corners in construction, such as direct bury of electrical cabling instead of running it through conduit. No matter how thick the sheathing on such cable may be, it will be subject to nicks and cracks over time, especially in areas prone to frost heave—and finding those problems and fixing them is hard work, expensive and disruptive. This also applies to water systems, which typically use plastic pipe of one sort or another—but thin-walled pipe is cheaper and more easily worked than sturdier thick-wall, and it's faster and cheaper to simply dig a trench, lay the pipe and then backfill, rather than prepping the trench with a sand or gravel foundation to cushion against ground movement.

Finding out how much care was exercised in choice of materials and installation of water and electric may be impossible, other than through conversation with the campground owner and his maintenance crew—if they know and if they're willing to be frank. But one revealing inquiry will be to ask how often the camp-ground has had to repair water leaks, as it's a rare campground that doesn't have any. You also should inspect the above-ground electric pedestals and water hydrants, which at the very least will give you a clue about the campground's overall commitment to quality. And while you're at it, ask how frequently the pedestals get serviced and how often the breakers—which get a *lot* of use—have been getting swapped out. If you're not confident about your abilities in this area, you should think about retaining a qualified electrician for an evaluation.

Meanwhile, even though the sewer system is mostly under-ground, it's also the most accessible of your buried utilities. If you hire only one professional tradesperson it should be from Roto-Rooter or a similar service, because these folks have cameras they can thread through the drains to look for collapsed pipes, root incursions or other problems that can quickly result in a major headache and potential health hazard. They also can inspect your septic tanks and drain fields, if you're not on a municipal system, and alert you to any shortcomings or impending issues with those, as well. (One pandemic-related alert on that score: because campground occupancy rates have increased so dramatically the past couple of years, the greater load on septic drain fields may exceed their design parameters and runs the risk of over-taxing them. That is most definitely not a problem you want to have to resolve.)

More work if you're not on municipal water/sewer

If the water distribution system is tied into a well, you'll want to know about that, too: how old and how deep it is, how many gallons a minute it will produce and how big a pump is on it. You'll want to know about the pump house, which should have one or more tanks to maintain water pressure when the pump is not running, as well as a chlorination pump or other disinfecting system. There undoubtedly will be a testing regimen you'll need to learn, including periodic sampling for E. coli and coliform bacteria, so ask about that—and while you're at it, find out what happens if the pump breaks or a power outage shuts it down. Is there more than one well on the property? If not, is there a back-up generator for the one, and how does that kick in? Is there a cistern or other water-storage tank, and how long can that supply meet anticipated need? In an emergency, how available is the nearest well technician?

(As the above descriptions may suggest, you'll have far fewer headaches if the campground is on a municipal water and sewer system, but many campgrounds almost by definition are outside such service areas. You nevertheless should ask if there's even a chance that municipal service could be extended to the property.)

Campground wi-fi, until recently regarded as an amenity on a par with cable TV, has unquestionably become the fourth utility. This was already becoming true before the pandemic, but the subsequent explosion of remote work has made a robust wi-fi system as essential in an RV park as 50-amp power. Ideally, it should be available everywhere in the campground and have a minimum download speed of 5 Mb per second, although 25 Mb is preferable. Check this out by roaming around the campground with a laptop and running periodic speed tests to see what the campers are experiencing. Find out how internet service is provided to the campground and whether it can be increased, or whether there are alternative providers.

You'll also want to assess the campground's roads and their condition, as well as all its buildings. If the roads are gravel—usually more common than asphalt, especially among older campgrounds—how much maintenance do they require? Are they well crowned, or do they have a lot of puddling in wet weather, resulting in more frequent potholes? How much gravel does the campground buy each year, and how is it applied? How often do the roads get graded, and what grading equipment does the campground have? What does it do about dust control in dry weather?

In examining the campground's various structures, you may be wise to retain a building inspector and an exterminator. You'll want to know the age and condition of all the roofs, whether electrical and plumbing installations are up to code—always a question among campgrounds marked by a DIY approach—and whether there's any sign of termite damage or rodent infestation. Look for indications of settling, such as cracked foundations or concrete pads, especially in buildings on hillsides.

Once you've poked and prodded as much as is reasonably possible (see Appendix B for a comprehensive due diligence checklist), you'll have to decide whether you've found anything that is a deal-breaker. Some issues may be out of the seller's control, or too nebulous to be properly evaluated, prompting you to walk away from the deal: problems with the title, legal threats of one kind or another, impending regulatory changes. Others may be more correctable, but too expensive or difficult for you to undertake—in which case, it's reasonable to ask the seller if he's willing to fix them before a sale is consummated. Still others will be things you'll be willing to accept, even if grudgingly, as the price of completing the transaction.

Whatever your final decision, you must communicate it to the seller by the agreed-upon deadline or risk losing your deposit. If you're prepared to move forward, on the other hand, you'll now have a pretty small window to reach closing—so gear up!   ❧

Chapter 6:
To Closing — and Beyond

IF YOU'VE GOTTEN THIS FAR: Congratulations! That means you've satisfied yourself—as best you can—that your proposed acquisition is in serviceable condition and not under any legal cloud, and you've met the deadline for notifying the owner that the sale is a go. But now you've got a lot of business to take care of, in the two weeks to a month before closing: you're not just buying a piece of land, but a business, and that means a lot of number crunching. It also means you have at least three groups of people who have to be eased into the ownership transition: vendors, employees and customers.

If your seller has not already done so, he should now provide you with a complete list of vendors and employees, as well as any contracts with members of either group. In most cases, the seller should make first contact with vendors to inform them of the impending ownership change and the closing date; this is especially critical for utilities, to ensure there isn't a gap in service—the last thing you want is for your campers to abruptly lose their electricity. You also need assurance that any disputes the seller may have with vendors are resolved before closing, and that there are no past-due bills.

Once the seller has notified his campground insurance company, you will need to follow up with your own application and premium payment so your closing agent can receive a binder prior to the sale being finalized. You might want to shop around for a different insurer, or you might want to adjust the terms of the existing policy, but my advice—barring any red flags that leap out at you—is that you simply maintain the status quo until you have more time and experience. In fact, I'll urge you to take a "go-slow" approach to making any changes until you've gotten your feet wet, a theme explored more in Chapter 7.

The seller also should arrange for the electric company to read the campground meters as close to the closing date as possible, and after that call is made, you'll have to set up your own account. The big shocker here may be the amount of deposit you'll be required to pay. Deposit policies and amounts vary from one utility to another, but at the extreme may be high enough to cover your campground's single largest monthly electric bill, which easily can run into several thousand dollars. On the other hand, you should explore other possibilities: when we bought our campground, we had a payment history as homeowners with another Virginia utility, and if we were willing to put the campground account in our personal names, rather than a corporate one, that history was enough to waive the deposit.

Similar calls should be made by the seller to the telephone company, the cable TV provider (if any) and the internet provider, followed by your application to switch those services without interruption. Your sales agreement should specify that the campground will continue using the same telephone numbers, email addresses and website addresses, but the providers may require the seller to confirm that by signing their authorization forms. You also should check with the campground's reservation system provider and its credit card processor to determine what you'll need to do to take over those accounts. As with the insurance company, it's best for now to stay with existing providers.

Other service providers you may have to contact include the trash hauler and the local municipality, if your campground gets city water and sewer. You should find out who's hosting the campground website and make sure that will transfer without a problem. If there are tradespeople with whom the campground deals on a regular basis, such as an electrician or HVAC service company, a courtesy call wouldn't be a bad idea.

A word about vendors . . .

This also is the time to contact the campground's supply vendors to let them know about the change of ownership, to learn if they've been on an automatic delivery schedule, and to find out about establishing your own credit accounts. Automatic deliveries might be scheduled for ice and propane, for example, while additional suppliers might provide ice cream, potato chips or other grocery items; in some cases, the campground may sell coffee, slushees, pizzas or other prepared foods that require a specific product delivery. Inquire also about the campground's accounts with local hardware stores, gardening supply centers and nurseries.

If you are inheriting a soda supplier, typically Coca Cola or Pepsi Cola, a couple of cautionary notes are in order. The two cola behemoths, each of which carries an extensive line of other soda products, will be happy to give you (i.e. let you use, not own) coolers and vending machines at no cost, which is easily a thousand bucks you won't have to shell out to buy your own. In exchange for this generosity, however, you'll have to agree to stock only their products and not the competition's—and as you'll soon learn, that's going to tick off whichever cola-loyal group of campers is left out. If you decide nonetheless to go with one or the other, make sure you understand the vendor's minimum stocking requirements and return policy, or risk ending a busy summer season with too many unreturnable cases of soda that reach their sell-by date in the middle of winter.

. . . and many more words about employees

The period following your due diligence is also the time to become acquainted with your new employees. Have the seller provide you with a list of all employees and their job titles and duties, together with how much they're paid, the length of their workweek, how long they've been with the campground, and their living arrangements—either on the premises or off. The seller also should tell you of any positions that are unfilled, and why. Depending on the time of year, the campground may still be hiring—in which case, make sure you're involved in any upcoming job interviews and decision making. Or it may be that the seller has been unable to fill some jobs even well into peak season, in which case you should ask what recruiting methods have been used and what problems have been encountered.

Of your three primary constituencies—vendors, employees and customers—employees comprise the group that may be the most difficult to acquire and maintain. Partly that's because campground employment, as is true of the hospitality industry in general, offers low wages; partly that's because of the seasonal nature of most campground employment, so that even campgrounds open year-round typically have an off-season that requires—and can sustain—only a smaller staff. As a result, it can be extraordinarily difficult for campgrounds to find good workers, since the people you most want to hire will want more pay and steadier work than you can provide.

If the campground you're buying is relatively small—say, 50 sites or less—this is less of a problem than if you're buying something considerably larger. You also may be lucky enough to be acquiring a campground with a well-established workforce that keeps coming back, year after year, in which case you should buy the seller a beer to toast your good fortune. In most situations, however, you will be on a near-constant hunt for decent employees—which means you should evaluate the existing staff with an open and forgiving attitude: just as there is no perfect campground, there is no such thing as a perfect employee, and the lower down the wage scale you go, the more pronounced that fact.

As you sit down with each employee for a brief face-to-face, remember that they'll be sizing you up with some trepidation, so my advice is that you don't go into this first encounter with a laundry list of all the things you plan on doing once you own the place. As with the vendors, it's best to convey the notion that you'll be maintaining the status quo while you learn the ropes. If the first rule of owning a campground is that you have to be there, the second rule is that you shouldn't fix things that aren't broken—and at this point, glaring exceptions aside, you don't know what's broken.

In that first meeting, you should try to get a sense of each employee's background and suitability for the job he or she is doing, how they perceive the overall work environment, what they wish they could be doing differently and what, if anything, they see going undone that needs attention. You will find that some employees are going to be more invested in the campground than others: work-campers, for example, may already be looking forward to their next assignment, halfway across the country, and don't have any commitment to you beyond finishing out their term. For others—if you're really, really lucky—this is something they've been doing for several years, they love the property and their work, and they have tons of ideas for making things better. That may not always be a good thing, if in their enthusiasm these employees lose sight of who's the boss, but that's a far better problem than having a listless counterpart who's simply there to get a paycheck for as little work as possible.

I mentioned work-campers. There are, in fact, three major sources of employees, with work-campers becoming a growing mainstay of many campground payrolls; the other two are local residents and, at the opposite extreme, foreign students recruited to work the summers on J-1 visas. You've probably encountered this last group in any heavily touristed area, with squads of bright young men and women speaking accented English manning cash registers, waiting tables, cleaning bathrooms and public areas, operating amusement park rides and doing dozens of other mostly menial jobs to keep the tourists amused, fed and housed. But that encounter was most likely not recent, as the Covid-19 pandemic threw that whole program for a loop and will take years to recover.

Work-campers, a subject addressed in more detail in Chapter 7, also are a limited resource because of how far ahead they plan their stays. Although it's not impossible for you to find work-campers at any time of the year, you'll be wise to ask why any work-camper worth his salt is looking for a position in the middle of the season—and be doubly sure to check his or her references.

The bottom line, then, is that any holes in your new campground's workforce will have to be filled by shuffling the existing staff, if possible; by hiring new employees from the surrounding area, which presumably the campground seller has attempted, without success; or by you and whatever family members or other help you'll be bringing with you. Those are tough—if not impossible—alternatives, but the sooner you understand them the better.

As you evaluate your human resources, you also should review the conditions under which the employees are working, starting with any established employee policies and procedures. Except in the very smallest operations, the campground should have some kind of employee handbook for each position that spells out job requirements and duties, reporting relationships, expected and prohibited attire and behavior, and other workplace aspects, such as payroll frequency, sick leave and vacation time (if any), emergency procedures and so on. In reviewing these rules, figure out how they fit with your management style—as well as how thoroughly the existing workforce complies with them. For example, what does the handbook say about smoking or cellphone use while on the job—and what's the observable reality?

Evaluate your campers — and a rate increase

Your third constituency, the campers, is the most fluid but in many respects the most reliable. Demand for RV park sites far exceeds supply these days, which gives campground owners unprecedented latitude in the level of service they provide, the rates they charge and the rules and policies they establish and enforce. For example, staffing shortages have in some instances been met with severely curtailed office hours, with campers encouraged to make reservations and to check-in online. Similarly, strong demand has given campground owners the leeway to set stricter standards in such matters as the age of the RV they'll permit on their property, with owners of units that are more than a decade old (the typical cut-off point) forced into negotiations they weren't anticipating.

Regardless of how much demand there is, however, you'll want to analyze how it's has been distributed across the various kinds of sites found in most campgrounds. Any decent campground reservation system can generate occupancy reports and what are known in real estate circles as "rent-roll" reports, which will provide a list of future reservations and advance deposits. You should request copies of each so you can determine which sites have been in highest demand—and, conversely, which have been underutilized—and at what times. Once you've analyzed this information you'll be able to determine two things: whether you have a proper balance of site types, and whether you need to adjust rates up or down.

Redressing a site imbalance—for example, upgrading some 30-amp sites to 50-amps—will go on a backburner for the moment, since that's not something you can tackle while you're still in the acquisition stage. But in an exception to the advice I gave earlier—about resisting the impulse to start changing things as soon as you take over—the very best time to increase rates is right from the get-go. It's all about human psychology: people expect prices to go up when a property changes hands, and while there may be grumbling, there will be less of it now than later. Moreover, if the campground has been under the same ownership for quite some time, it almost invariably will not have raised prices at a rate commensurate with other campgrounds in the area—and many of the campers will know that, even if subconsciously.

So how do you know whether you should increase rates? One obvious barometer is the one I just mentioned—the other campgrounds in your area—whose rate schedules you should have gathered during your due diligence period. If most of your competitors are charging $60 a night for full-hook-up 50-amp pull-through sites and your campground is charging only $50, then that's a clue that you should think about an increase. Just make sure you're comparing apples to apples—don't mix up pull-through sites (which should charge more) with back-ins, or 50-amp sites (which should charge more) with 30 amps.

Another metric to review is your occupancy rates. If a certain set of sites—let's use the full hook-up 50-amp pull-throughs again, for consistency's sake—are getting booked 90% of the time or more, you're not charging enough. Raise the rates by an amount sufficient to more than off-set whatever dip in reservations results, creating room for campers who may have been unable to get in before. And not all the campers you scare away with the higher rates will go elsewhere—some will simply book a cheaper site, where your occupancy rates may have been lower. For more discussion about rate setting, see Chapter 9.

Finally, a rate increase, if warranted, is especially well-timed now for any long-term campers. Although you'll be bound by any long-term contractual agreements if you're in season, any month-to-month campers don't have a guaranteed rate beyond the end of their current 30-day period. And if you're in the off-season, before any seasonal campers have arrived, you're able to give them the option of agreeing to a higher rate or to get a refund. Assuming you don't get greedy, you'll mostly get the higher rate.

Prorations and purchase price allocations

In addition to evaluating your three major constituencies, this pre-closing interim is the time for settling various financial and bookkeeping affairs. Among them is the sometimes-tricky task of business prorations, with a percentage of prepays credited to the seller—the actual amount depending on the closing date—and advanced payments credited to the buyer. These amounts will be included in the closing statement itself, along with the closing costs, so that there will be only one consolidated transaction. For simplicity's sake, prorated amounts are usually calculated on a 30-day month and a 360-day year.

Prepaid items—expenses for which the seller has already paid but which typically cover an entire year—may include advertising the campground in directories or on web sites, as well as billboards and highway logo signs. Other prepays may include association memberships and dues, for example to the National Association of RV Parks and Campgrounds, or to the local Chamber of Commerce or a local tourist association; as well as various business licenses, including—at most campgrounds—ASCAP and BMI for playing music in a commercial setting, or the Motion Picture Licensing Corporation for the right to show movies. If the fees for these and similar items cover a calendar year, you'll be repaying the seller for that portion of the year following the closing date.

The campground also may have purchased propane or firewood for resale, so the seller will need to be reimbursed for the unsold portion of each. And the potentially biggest headache will be accounting for store inventory, which will be less of a headache if the seller has been using a point-of-sale system that allows rapid scanning of the unsold items. Lacking that, you and the seller will either have to go the tedious pen-and-paper route or, if you can agree, simply settle on a ballpark final estimate that both parties feel is reasonable.

On the flip side, you as the buyer will be owed any advance payments, such as deposits for reservations following the closing date. You'll also be owed the prorated amount of any prepaid camping fees, for instance, the amount paid for the balance of a seasonal camper's stay. If the seasonal rate is $2,100 and the season is seven months long, each month of the season that continues past the closing date should net you a $300 payment from the seller.

Another bookkeeping exercise that must be completed, sometimes during the due diligence period and in other cases at any time prior to closing, is something called the "allocation of purchase price." This seemingly arcane process, which simply divides the purchase price among several different categories, can become complicated because of the way it affects each party's tax situation—and at various times, as the tax code changes, what benefits the seller might (or might not) be detrimental to the buyer, and vice versa.

Among the typical asset categories, to which a greater or

lesser portion of the sales price will be allocated, are the land, the property's buildings and improvements, its equipment and fixtures, store and other inventory, and goodwill; additional categories, depending on the circumstances, may include a non-compete covenant (e.g. barring the seller from going into business with a new campground within a certain distance) and the value of a KOA or Jellystone franchise. Different asset categories are taxed at different rates that may vary from time to time, as well as having varying amortization or depreciation rates, which is why you—as well as the seller—will want an accountant's advice. If you're lucky, the stars will align and there won't be a lot of initial difference between the two sides, because buyer and seller must agree fully by closing.

Final bits and pieces

As you move through all of the above items on your to-do list, there will be any number of smaller, less critical but nonetheless important things needing your attention prior to closing. Here are a few of them:

• Make sure you get the original titles for all vehicles and mobile homes—including park models and cabins built on a chassis—that convey with the property, and be aware you may have to pay sales tax when re-registering them.

• Check to see if you're required to obtain training and licensing to operate certain park features, including a propane fill station, a swimming pool or a sewer plant, depending on the campground and the state you're in.

• If the current owner or his manager lives on the premises and you intend to occupy that dwelling, discuss and agree on when that turnover will occur and in what condition the home will be conveyed.

• Your payment at closing will be via wire transfer or certified check. But because final prorations will be done the day of closing, you may need to bring additional cash to cover a balance due—or gain the seller's permission beforehand to write a personal check. In past years that could run as high as $5,000, but with the recent trend toward more advance reservations, it's ever more likely that it will be the seller who will be making up any difference.

One final note. Your purchase agreement should include a provision obligating the seller to be on call to assist you in the two weeks following the sale, and possibly for another period later in the year, to show you first-hand how to operate various aspects of the campground. This may include day-to-day opening and closing of the swimming pool, routine testing of the waterworks as required by the health department, opening and closing of the store and registers, taking inventory and restocking the store, bookkeeping entries at each daily closing, payroll, and so on—anything that requires your attention on an ongoing basis. A second hands-on period will be helpful at the end of the season, when you'll need to know what systems have to be winterized and how that's best done. And you also should have a contractual right to reach out to him or her, for up to a year after closing, for advice, references or help with unexpected problems.

You may think you want this hand-holding period to last much longer than a mere two weeks, but trust me—you want to pick the seller's brain as thoroughly as you can and then ease him on his way. There should be no question in your employees' and your campers' minds that you are the new boss, and there should be no opportunity for the seller to overshadow you, even if inadvertently or unintentionally. Take lots of pictures and copious notes. If absolutely necessary, use the phone or email to get the answers you need.

Once you've checked off all the above, you're ready to request copies of your closing documents. Take care to review them carefully before showing up at escrow to sign all the paperwork—and to get your keys, original vehicle titles and other documents. Jubilation is in order—tempered with the realization that your life is about to be turned upside down. ✌

Getting down to businesss

Chapter 7:
Taking Stock

AT SOME POINT YOU WILL BE STRUCK by the awful/wonderful realization that the brass ring you've been chasing for the past year or more is actually in your grasp. You've signed your papers, you've paid your money and now, for better or worse, you've acquired a whole mess of responsibilities that may be unlike any you've shouldered before. It's daunting!

But first, take a breath. Take the time to stroll around your property. Savor the views, for surely there are some; wave to campers and staff; admire the complex interplay of physical features, utilities and manmade amenities that have transformed this piece of dirt into a refuge for city dwellers, young families, retirees and nomads of all ages. You'll need to recall these initial, heartfelt impressions in the months and years ahead, when the all-consuming nature of the task you've undertaken threatens to beat you down and make you forget why you got into this business in the first place.

If you've owned a business before, you're aware of many of the burdens you've accepted. There are employees, of course, which means payroll and scheduling and dealing with the personal crises that inevitably threaten to derail your plans. There are vendors and tradespeople, who may or may not be counted upon to deliver what you need when you need it. And there are the "customers," who are much more complex in their demands than mere store patrons or hotel guests or heavy-equipment operators—who are, in fact, a combination of all those things, and who therefore will pull and tug at you in various directions simultaneously.

But unless you've also been a farmer or a golf course supervisor or a home builder, your prior business experience has probably left you unprepared for the physical and infrastructure demands of this new venture. You are, first of all, at the mercy of the elements. "Getting back to nature" loses its charm for many people when nature is wet or cold, not only prompting cancellations of advance reservations but often resulting in demands for refunds from campers who've decided they want to cut their visits short. You'll want to think about how you'll deal with such requests, a topic examined more closely in Chapter 9.

Meanwhile, nature in its less appealing aspects can take a toll on the campground itself. If you have water features, like a lake or streams, there's the ever-present threat of flooding. Heavy winds or ice storms can bring down trees or multiple limbs. Tornadoes can take out buildings and more trees, and even distant forest fires can cause problems with air quality. Invasive insects can wipe out all of one or another tree species, while termites and carpenter ants may happily munch on bathhouses and cabins. Larger wildlife in all its many forms, from Canada geese to skunks to brown bears and raccoons, may make you and your campers miserable with their poop and smells and scavenging.

Meanwhile, the infrastructure that transforms your piece of dirt into a pastoral retreat is almost certainly far more fragile than you know. Underground electrical cable, more often than not, has been buried directly rather than being threaded through conduit, making it vulnerable to nicks and breaks from frost heave below and compression from RVs rolling above. Ditto for plastic water mains, which in addition to similar vulnerabilities have the added stress of freezing and thawing if not properly winterized. Hydrants and electric pedestals are vulnerable to being clipped— or even flattened—by RVers with bigger rigs than they know how to handle; so are fences, trees and virtually anything else sticking out of the ground.

All of which is to say that buying a campground is in many respects far easier than actually running one—not that you can't do it. But it helps if you approach this next phase of your life with two essential qualities: organizational skills, and humility.

A little humility will pay big dividends

Let's start with humility, since that's often in rare supply. As already mentioned in a previous chapter, I strongly advise you to take things slow until you've had a chance to get your feet wet. You may have all kinds of ideas of how things can be improved or what needs to be changed, and a lot of those ideas may be perfectly swell. But take it from me that there's a reason why things are the way they are—and until you know what that reason is, you risk "fixing" something that isn't broken.

That isn't to say that things can't be done differently; there almost always is more than one route to a destination, and the reason for things being the way they are is not always the best. I'm also not saying you shouldn't step in when there's an obvious hazard or seriously deficient practice. But keep in mind that the way things are currently organized has been working for a while, and so presumably may be expected to keep working until you get your bearings. A couple of examples from a campground I know, one seemingly trivial and one very consequential, may illustrate my point.

In the first case, the new owner decided shortly after arriving to move a small portable sign that had been placed in front of a 30-foot aluminum flagpole near the campground entrance. What he didn't realize was that the flagpole was in the path of people backing out of a parking space, and even though there was adequate space for such a maneuver, two flagpoles had already been destroyed by careless drivers with a heavy foot on the accelerator. The seller therefore had placed a portable sign several feet in front of the flagpole as a visual and aural warning to anyone backing up too far. Guess what happened within a couple of weeks after the buyer moved the sign?

Thirty-foot commercial-grade flagpoles aren't cheap, but you can argue that moving the sign was an easily made mistake. Perhaps. Consider, then, the buyer's equally hasty decision to dredge a small lake on the property—in itself a major undertaking—and furthermore, to have the job done by his newly acquired maintenance crew operating a rented dredge. There's little question that the dredging was needed, but the way it was undertaken was less than optimal, as the new owner quickly demonstrated that he had no clear idea of his employees' abilities, or of the amount of dredging spoil that would be involved, or of the time it would take for either the dredging or the subsequent dewatering—an essential step before the spoil could be hauled away.

Consequently, a job that should have started in November and wrapped up before mid-December's freezes didn't start until January. The late start, combined with turnover on the maintenance crew and its inexperience, meant the dredging was still underway in April, so that the dewatering bags were still draining a month later, when the new camping season was well underway. Since the dewatering bags had been spread across several RV sites, the late start meant the loss of revenue those sites would have brought in. And because of the late start and slow dredging progress, campers could be entertained early that summer with the beeping and gear-grinding of a parade of dump trucks and backhoes at work hauling off the spoils.

All of which is to say, a lot of unnecessary expense and loss of goodwill can be avoided by recognizing your limitations. Be humble enough to know what you don't know—and to reach out to those who do.

Discipline is humility's handmaiden

In addition to benefiting from an injection of humility, a lot of real and potential problems will become much more manageable if tackled in a disciplined, structured way. What that means is a) prioritize what needs to be done; b) make a realistic plan for tackling a task, taking into consideration the time, manpower and materials you'll need; c) factor in the weather you're likely to encounter, since most of the jobs you'll be undertaking will be outside; and d) finish one task before starting another.

This last point can't be stressed enough: it's dismaying how many "improvements" I've seen at campgrounds that never quite got finished, usually because some other project was calling and the incomplete one seemed "good enough" for now and could always be completed later—only "later" never arrived. This kind of attention deficit disorder is comparable to an otherwise well-crafted car that nevertheless suffers from poor "fit and finish" —the doors that aren't hung evenly, leaving a gap that is wider at the top than the bottom. Or the paint job that blisters or peels after a few years. Attention to detail is critical, and people notice when it's not there.

A real-life example to make the point: a campground with 12 cabins, all of which but one received a new coat of stain before cold weather prevented completing the job. The twelfth cabin should have been stained as soon as returning spring weather made that possible—but by then, the campground manager was so used to seeing it a certain way that he no longer recognized that it was sticking out like a sore thumb. One comment that should have tipped him off, but didn't, came from a camper reserving a cabin for a future stay. Told he would be getting the cabin that hadn't been stained, he asked if he couldn't have the "newer" one next door—even though both cabins were the exact same age.

Attention to detail. Fit and finish. People notice.

You already should have a fair grasp of the deferred maintenance that awaits you, as well as some relatively minor improvements that can be knocked out easily, from your due diligence observations and initial questioning of employees about their sense of what needs to be done. If you didn't ask those questions during the inspection period, do so now. Also take the time to walk around the campground with a critical eye, before familiarity and routine dull your observations, looking for the incomplete, the unkempt and the ignored. At our campground, for example, I noticed early on that none of the buildings other than the office and main bathhouse had gutters—and as a result, campers stepping out of a rental cabin in the rain had to plunge through a stream of water cascading from the pitched roof. That was a relatively easy fix for a major nuisance.

Indeed, when it comes to cabins—and it's becoming rare for a campground not to have any, and usually several—it's not a bad idea to spend one or more nights in each to get a first-hand lesson in what works and what doesn't. Sleep in the bed, cook in the kitchen, shower in the bathroom—you may get some eye-opening surprises, from uncomfortable mattresses to an inferior quality of cutlery to a shockingly limited supply of hot water. Some you can readily fix, like upgrading to a better mattress or higher quality silverware and pots and pans; others, like the hot water supply, may be more difficult to remedy: a bigger hot water tank (in which case, will it fit?)? Or maybe an "insta-hot" replacement for the traditional water heater (but is your water too hard for that to be feasible?)?

At the very least, you'll learn enough from your first-hand experience to let your guests know of possible issues ahead of time, for which they—and you—ultimately will be grateful. People will take a lot of things in stride if forewarned, but will turn on you in a heartbeat if their expectations aren't otherwise met. Indeed, this might be the right place to note the third cardinal rule of running a campground (or, for that matter, managing any hospitality business): Always under-promise and over-deliver, not the other way around.

What you're determining from these more detailed inspections is what needs to be done to fix what's already there—to turn what's shabby into something polished, to oil what's squeaky and to trim what's overgrown. This is not the time to be implementing a grocery list of new ideas and amenities, accumulated from reading and visiting other campgrounds and daydreaming about putting your personal stamp on a property that's been around ten or 20 or 50 years before you ever rolled onto the scene. There'll be time for that later, I assure you. But if you don't want to make a complete hash of things, my advice is that you first understand what you've got before you take it to some whole new level.

Employees—the elephant in the room

Unless you've acquired a pretty small campground, your to-do list isn't going anywhere without employees to do much of the work—and oh, boy, is that a kettle of fish! Finding and retaining good employees will be one your biggest headaches, and as difficult as that was before the pandemic, it's now three times worse. If you're stepping into the business mid-season and you have a full payroll roster, great! But if you have openings you need to fill immediately, or if a substantial number of your current employees can't be expected to return next year, this will be one of the first issues you'll need to address.

Traditionally, you have three labor pools to draw from: local workers, overseas students, and work campers. The skills, availability and requirements for each are in constant flux, so what's true in any one moment may look entirely different six months later—you'll have to be nimble. Moreover, the lead time and stability of each labor pool varies considerably: local workers, at one extreme, are immediately available (if you can find them) but are as readily able to walk out the door if they find a better opportunity elsewhere, or don't like the job—or don't like you. Foreign students, at the other extreme, have to be lined up at least six months in advance—but once they're on the premises, their options are limited. Work campers, meanwhile, fall in the middle of this range.

Regardless of where you find your workers, however, it's critical for your long-term success that you regard them as assets, not as grudgingly tolerated drains on your bottom line. Although employees are treated as an expense on a profit and loss statement, you should guard against having that utilitarian perspective bleed into your day-to-day attitude toward the people you need to make your campground profitable. It's simply good business to treat employees as valuable assets (unless they're not, in which case yes, show them the door), which means treating them with respect and an understanding that they also have ideas, complaints, frustrations and needs—just like you!

And guess what? Your employees are realizing that, too. Although much has been made of the post-pandemic Great Resignation, it's worth noting that not everyone is experiencing the same amount of pain—and your kind of business has been hit harder than any other. Indeed, the national quit rate for workers in the accommodation and food services sector—which includes campgrounds and RV parks—was averaging 6% a month through the latter part of 2021 and beginning of 2022. That means a quarter of all employees were jumping ship every four months—more than in any other industry sector, and twice the overall national rate.

Driving this exodus have been miserably low wages, dismissive employer attitudes and grinding work with few personal rewards. But for a large segment of the campground industry it's even worse than that, because so many RV parks are either closed for a chunk of each year or have to pare back their workforce significantly in the off-season. In other words, you're in the position of trying to attract and retain employees for positions that historically pay at or near the minimum wage in exchange for low-skilled but often boring or repetitive work that may last only six or seven months. Where do you find people like that, and how do you make them want to work for you?

Start by reviewing pay rates and benefits

Let's start by recognizing that the old ways are changing, and for the better. A decade ago, you could get by with paying most of your employees at or just a bit above the federal minimum wage—which has been stuck at $7.25 an hour going all the way back to 2009. Think about how little that can buy these days. To maintain spending power, that wage of $7.25 in 2012 should be $9.59 in 2022, but even at that level it wouldn't be enough to put a roof over one's head and food in one's belly.

Many campground owners, recognizing that they were in fact paying far less than a living wage, justified their miserliness by claiming that they were hiring mostly high school kids, not family heads, but that was a bogus response on at least two levels: first, it largely wasn't true; and second, even if it were true, so what? The appropriate index is a job's worth, not what you can get away with paying. And the less you pay, the more you signal how little you value the work that's being done, a lesson won't be lost on your employees. (Historical aside: one of the wry comments made by workers in the former Soviet Union about their state economy was, "They pretend to pay us, and we pretend to work.")

The pandemic and the Great Resignation have goosed state minimum wages into the low teens all around the country, even as the federal minimum has remained stubbornly unchanged. The U.S. Office of Personnel Management, on the other hand, announced at the beginning of 2022 that federal civilian employees in the U.S. will now be paid at least $15 an hour, and although that doesn't apply to private employers like you, I'll strongly advise you to follow suit. Offer less of a starting wage and you're likely to find yourself spinning your wheels, advertising positions for which you'll get either no applicants or, worse yet, applicants no one else wants.

Assuming you follow my advice, you'd better also review the pay rates of existing employees—and be prepared to make adjustments. You may have inherited staffers with several years at the campground who are making $10 or $12 or even $15 an hour without a murmur of discontent, but let them see you looking to fill positions for a wage at or above what they're making and you'll have a mutiny on your hands. The adage about a rising tide lifting all boats applies to labor markets as well. And while it may seem, at first blush, that raising wages will seriously dent profit margins, the fact is that an average 20% wage increase (to toss out an example) will make a huge difference for your employees but increase your overall operating expenses by a quarter to one-third of that ratio. You can make that up with only a nominal rate increase.

There are other ingredients to throw into this hopper. The biggest one is health care, which larger operations than yours often can provide through a group insurance plan, but which you probably can't afford. As an alternative, figure out what you can afford, per employee—be it $200 a month, $350 or more—and offer to chip that in toward the premium of a program offered through the Affordable Care Act. Or offer up to that same amount to help defray the cost of a spouse's employer plan, which frequently provides family coverage only at a stiff premium over single coverage.

To encourage safe workplace behavior, consider defraying the cost of workplace boots for maintenance and grounds crews, and perhaps for housekeepers. Be prepared also to provide work gloves (leather for maintenance, nitryl or latex for housekeeping), and to offer face masks, safety glasses and ear protection for anyone working with caustic chemicals or power machinery. For much the same reason, make sure employees have ready access to as much drinking water as they want.

And think about how you might structure a sick leave policy—especially for employees who are in regular contact with co-workers and campers, such as desk staff—and whether you can create a work schedule that gives employees regular days off. Neither sick-leave policies nor regular days off have been standard fare at campgrounds, and even less so as employee ranks have been thinned the past couple of years, but the times are a changin' and your campground should, too.

Looking overseas for campground workers

In addition to hiring locally, you also can look to hire from overseas or from the large—and apparently growing—pool of work campers. Keep in mind, however, that both these sources need more advance planning, each has its own limitations, and neither is a panacea.

The first option, made less reliable because of the pandemic and its attendant travel restrictions, as well as growing international tensions, comprises two federal programs designed specifically to serve seasonal employers. The more difficult to tap into is the H-2B visa program, administered by the U.S. Department of Labor, which each year admits seasonal workers for up to six months at a time for employers like landscapers, fisheries, resorts and vacation-town vendors. The number of such visas is capped by Congress—in recent years at 66,000, but with an additional 64,000 visas authorized annually in response to market conditions—but involves a significant amount of paperwork that will deter most small employers.

Among the hurdles: if you want to hire someone under the H-2B program, you must first demonstrate there's a lack of suitable workers locally by advertising the jobs you need filled, including with your state unemployment office. The local recruitment effort must be at a standard wage that is determined by the federal government's statistics for comparable positions—a rate you may find higher than anticipated. And the government is not going to find your temporary workers for you—you'll have to do that yourself. Employers who already have large numbers of H-2B workers have a built-in recruitment network: it's called family connections. You won't be so lucky.

Given the H-2B program's complexities, most campground owners who hire overseas workers do so through the entirely separate J-1 student visa program, which is administered by the U.S. State Department. Designed as a cultural immersion opportunity, the J-1 program is promoted as a chance for college students to spend their summer vacations earning some money, improving English-speaking skills, and being exposed to American history, culture and landmarks. For employers, the program is an opportunity to hire bright young people who are eager to work for them at jobs that many American college students would hesitate to take, such as housekeeping, for wages older workers would decline. Moreover, J-1 students are a "captive" work force, unable like their American counterparts to simply walk off the job.

That said, the J-1 workforce has unique requirements and

limitations that may deter you. Because it is in fact a cultural immersion program, employers must commit to providing at least one cultural activity per month. That almost certainly will mean a guided or chaperoned outing, which will require you to devote time—yours or a trusted surrogate's—to a non-workplace activity. Because the foreign students are non-local, you'll have to ensure adequate housing—a requirement that could put this option out of your reach, although one possible solution would be to buy one or more travel trailers that can be rented out to campers when they're not being used for employee housing. And because the students are here on their summer vacations, that usually means they're available for only three to four months, typically between June or July into late September or early October, depending on country of origin.

(A caution: before the pandemic derailed the J-1 program, there was some discussion at the State Department about limiting or even banning use of RVs for student housing. If you decide to participate in the program and plan on using travel trailers or fifth-wheels for accommodations, you should ask your program sponsor if federal guidance on this point has changed.)

On the plus side, J-1 employers don't have to do a lot of heavy lifting at the front end. Students are recruited by a dozen or more State Dept.-certified "sponsors" that act as brokers, matching program applicants with employers based on interviews and questionnaires filled out by both parties. You'll describe job duties, pay rate and what kind of living accommodations you'll provide; the students will indicate what kinds of jobs they're looking for, what part of the U.S. they want to work in, and biographical details about their work experience, college studies and English proficiency. There won't be any cost to you—the students pay all agency fees as well as their transportation costs—but you'll be limited to accepting or declining the candidates presented for your review, although you will get the opportunity to conduct a Zoom interview.

Unfortunately, depending on how many J-1 students you're seeking as well as where you're located, the pickings may be slim. Many sponsors find it economically unrewarding to deal with employers who want less than a handful of students, when there are mega-employers—think any major tourist attraction, like the Wisconsin Dells or the Virginia shore—that need dozens and even hundreds of workers each. And many J-1 applicants aren't looking for a two-bit RV park tucked away in some obscure corner of the landscape—they want to be near one of the country's major cities or natural landmarks, like Yosemite or Mount Rushmore.

That said, there are recruiting agencies that will work with even the smallest employers—you'll just have to persist. One place to start is here: *https://j1visa.state.gov/participants/how-to-apply/ sponsor-search/?program=Summer%20Work%20Travel.*

Work-campers—a mixed blessing

The third labor pool that you can tap into is the growing army of work-campers, sometimes also written as "workampers," a subject already broached at the tail end of Chapter 2 as one way for you to get acquainted with the campground industry. There's no need to repeat that information here, but there are a few additional considerations you should keep in mind when you're the employer, not the employee.

The first is that work-campers will, by definition, require an RV site—one with full hook-ups and, in all likelihood, a 50-amp pedestal—that will come out of your most profitable inventory of income producers. Keeping that in mind, you'll want to assign any work-campers to the campgound's least desirable options, such as sites that are difficult to back into or that are located too close to a bathhouse, busy road or other unattractive feature.

The second is the possibility that the wrong work-campers will run right over you, especially if they sense that you're still figuring things out. Most of them have been doing this for a while, they know the business, and depending on personality type may feel things at your campground should be done their way. This is exactly the reason why you didn't want the former owner to hang around for more than a couple of weeks, and you should just as firmly draw the line with people who are, after all, working for you, not the other way around.

The third, perhaps most significant thing to keep in mind is that work-campers can leave at the drop of a hat. They rolled into your campground in their house on wheels, and they can roll out just as readily—and will, if they feel put upon or if a better offer comes along. Moreover, if you're hiring a couple—as is often the case, because campground owners figure they'll get two workers in exchange for losing only one RV site—you risk losing two workers even if only one is unhappy. Given the presumed size of your campground, that could put a major dent in your labor supply.

One possible preventative: a compensation package that includes a bonus of $1 to $2 an hour for every hour worked that season—provided the work-camper is still on payroll at the end of his or her contract. Although no guarantee of employee stability, that's enough to give most people second-thoughts about pulling a vanishing act, and even more so as the bonus grows with each passing week. ❧

Chapter 8:
The Changing Face of the Camping Public

IF THERE'S ONE THING in the past few years that has upended the campground industry more than any other, it's the campers themselves.

It wasn't all that long ago that anthropologists Dorothy Ayers Counts and David R. Counts were able to carve out a professional niche for themselves by studying a largely unexamined subculture, comprising "RVing seniors in trailer parks, 'boondocking' sites on government land, laundromats, and other meeting places across the continent." Their 2001 ethnography, *Over The Next Hill*, was the first serious examination of what we now describe as "full-timers," or retirees who had decided to live out the rest of their lives on the road, and thereby held up for public review a lifestyle that had largely escaped notice.

"They do not spend their days sitting on their porches in their rocking chairs or baking cookies in hope their grandchildren will drop by," the couple described their subjects in the book's introduction. "Instead they are out roaming the blue highways, sleeping in truck stops, parking in the desert for months at a time. These old folks are not acting like old folks used to! What is going on here? What are these seniors telling us about the concept of aging in North America?"

What, indeed? And what were they saying about a deeper wanderlust in the American character? In the ten years following publication of *Over The Next Hill*, the industry cranked out 3 million RVs—and in the decade after that, nearly 4.5 million more. Once perceived as a vaguely sketchy lifestyle, RVing exploded into public awareness as an attractive way for families to vacation, for people of all ages to explore the outdoors, and for retirees to live not as itinerant travelers but as seasonal migrants, moving south in the winter and north in the summer—as "snowbirds." And then the pandemic hit like a ton of bricks, and suddenly RVing was also embraced as an alternative lifestyle by even the most buttoned-down office workers.

What this means for you is two-fold. First, it means demand for camping spaces has never been higher, as the supply of RV sites simply has not kept pace with the number of RVers seeking a berth. And second, it means that the mix of campers has never been greater: those grey-haired retirees are still out there, of course, but so are families with kids, single or coupled professionals working out of their RVs, young people looking for outdoor adventures, plus the usual potpourri of iconoclasts, misanthropes, and borderline hermits who always have been attracted to life on the road.

Take a closer look, and you'll realize that each of these customer segments has needs and expectations that not only aren't universally shared, but which often will conflict with one another. Older RVers may have little patience for screaming kids. Families with children are going to want playgrounds and organized activities that others will grouse about as unnecessarily increasing everyone's site fees. White-collar professionals will need reliable wi-fi that may get bogged down by teenagers streaming movies— and on and on. What you'll soon realize is that your campground can't be all things to all people—and, fortunately, that the overall increase in demand allows you to be somewhat selective in the kind of campers you'll seek out. Your job is to figure out who they are—and how to get them.

Some of this was addressed in Chapter 3, and hopefully you took that discussion to heart when setting your criteria for the kind of campground you'd be acquiring. To use the most obvious example, it's too late now for you to decide you really don't like kids if the campground you bought is a Jellystone. In the real world, however, few campgrounds are all one type or another, and it's going to be up to you to decide if the blend you currently have works for you, or if you need to adjust it somehow. The following discussion addresses some of your possible choices.

Do you want year-round or seasonal guests?

Many—perhaps most—campgrounds until recently had a mix of transient and long-term campers. The transient guests would bring in more money, because nightly rates were always two to three times higher than the prorated nightly rate for monthly or longer stays. Month-to-month or seasonal campers, on the other hand, were desirable because they smoothed out the revenue curve, providing income at times when the transient traffic would dry up. Month-to-month campers pay every four weeks, right through the off-season; seasonals pay in two or more installments in the winter for the following summer, ensuring themselves a space while injecting much needed cash in the slowest part of the year.

As demand for RV spaces has heated up, however, a growing number of campgrounds is cutting back or completely eliminating such stays. Campers are always free to reserve as many nights as they want, of course—but without the discounts associated with seasonal stays. So, for example, a full hook-up site that might sell for $60 a night may have been available for a three-month seasonal reservation for $1,500 to $2,500—or $17 to $28 a night for the 90 days. Yet that same site booked at a nightly rate will pull in $2,700 at just 50% occupancy—and 50% these days looks like a snap. The same logic applies to month-to-month rentals.

As a result, long-term stays—if even available at a particular campground—have become increasingly expensive. A monthly rate of $500, which wasn't unusual pre-pandemic, these days will have doubled or more at many RV parks, and even at that level will be offering a significant discount to the daily rate. Some campgrounds, on the other hand, have instituted relatively minor increases in their monthly rates but only offer them in the off-season, such as Nov. 1 to April 30, or Dec. 1 to March 31, after which the sites must be vacated. Such campgrounds also tend not to have seasonal sites at all. One consequence of all this is that using an RV as a summer vacation retreat is becoming increasingly rare; another is that RVs are becoming increasingly untenable as a cheap housing alternative.

You'll have to think about these factors when you evaluate the current distribution of sites at your campground and whether you want to change the balance. There is, however, one additional set of variables you should consider, and that's the nature of the sites themselves. Just as you'd be foolish to put long-term campers on your longest pull-through sites, since those are the ones you have the least trouble filling, you'd be foolish to shoe-horn transient guests into sites that are too small or too close to a dumpster or heavily traveled road. Not only will those transient campers be unhappy—and all the more so if they look around at the much nicer sites they weren't able to get—but they'll make you unhappy by scorching you on social media.

It may be that your campground was built within the past ten years by someone who knew what he was doing, in which case none of this applies. But the unfortunate reality in most cases is that some of your sites just aren't as desirable as others, and those are the ones you should set aside for long-term campers, at least until you're able to correct their deficiencies. At the campground my wife and I owned, for example, there were some perfectly fine sites that nonetheless were so hard to back into, because of the lay of the land, that assigning them to transient campers would have meant no end of frustration for them and damaged property for us. Those all became month-to-month sites. We also had a much older section of the campground that provided one shared pedestal and one common hydrant for every two sites—which meant some RVers needed 40 feet of electrical cable to reach the outlet, and a similar length of water hose. Those, too, became month-to-month sites, as someone staying long-term would be less resistant than an over-nighter to the idea of buying a 20-foot extension cable.

How long do you want campers to stay?

Even if you don't have designated long-term sites—but especially if you do—you should think about how long you want your campers to stay. As discussed in Chapter 3, an RV park dominated by a lot of long-term campers can quickly take on a personality determined by them, not you, and not always to your liking. But even a small proportion of long-term campers can cause problems by developing an excessive sense of ownership, which is only natural—we all tend to feather our nests to our own liking.

There are two ways to discipline this inclination so it doesn't become overwhelming. One is to have an explicit and detailed set of rules that set out the boundaries of acceptable behavior for your long-term campers. This could range from prohibiting (or limiting) additions, such as porches, storage sheds and decks, to specifying how many guests can stay in the RV and for how long, to establishing the number and kinds of vehicles that may be parked at the site. Without these and other restrictions you run the risk of having the site overrun with non-registered visitors and various vehicles, resulting in its gradual degradation.

The other controlling factor is to have time limits. You'll notice, for example, that I've been referring to "month-to-month" campers instead of the more obvious "monthlies," and that's for a couple of reasons. One is that using the phrase "month-to-month" emphasizes—for both you and the camper—that this is not an open-ended situation: that in fact the RVer is making a brand-new reservation each month and not simply extending a reservation made three or six months ago. The end of each month becomes a new decision point: by you, as to whether you want to have that RVer stay another 30 days, and by the RVer, deciding if he or she wants to stay or go. Having that short timeline focuses everybody's attention in a way that's lost when the relationship between camper and campground stretches into some indefinite future.

Limiting your campers to 30-day windows, even if those windows are strung together over a year or more, also helps you dodge the legal pitfall of entering a landlord-tenant relationship. As the owner of a campground with short-term guests, you have a legally enforceable right to throw out campers who don't comply with your rules, who harass other guests or who are just plain obnoxious—and if they fail to comply, you have a right to call the local sheriff to enforce your decision, on threat of being arrested for trespassing. Once you enter a landlord-tenant relationship, however, most states have lengthy notification periods and numerous legal hurdles you have to clear before you can get rid of someone.

Confused? You're not alone, but think of it this way: your campground should be viewed by campers, law enforcement officers and all others as being more similar to a hotel than to an apartment building. Your guests are transients, even if it's for 30 days, so when you eject them—not "evict" them, which is landlord-tenant language—you are removing their property (trailer, fifth-wheel or other RV) from your property. You are not throwing people out of their home, but instead requiring them to move their home.

This distinction should carry over into the language you use and some of the policies you implement. As a seemingly extreme example, an attorney who works on behalf of ARVC recommends you shouldn't say you're "leasing" an RV site, but rather that you're "licensing" it for a specific "license term." While that may seem like an awkward description, you should at least refrain from referring to site payments as "rent"—"fees" will do quite nicely. Meanwhile, it's prudent for you to prohibit your campers from using the campground address for their mail deliveries, which in addition to creating many headaches for you after they leave, gives them ammunition for claiming residency. Tell them to get a local post office mailbox instead, or at the very least, to have any mail sent "in care of" the campground.

Even 'transient' guests need time limits

It's not only long-term Rvers who need time limits. It's an unfortunate sign of the times that a growing number of people are unable to find affordable housing and are casting about for any plausible substitute. Some may scrape together enough money to buy a beat-up old RV and move around from one campground to another, paying for one or two nights at a time; others, with even more meager resources, may resort to living in tents. Still others will inquire about renting cabins for one or more weeks, until the money runs out.

These can be extremely difficult situations to confront, because the people in them are so obviously doing the best they can with little to no financial resources and little hope of improving their situation. On the other hand, you're in no position to apply means-testing for your would-be campers, nor should you, even though you have an obvious interest in maintaining a welcoming environment for everyone and ensuring that some campers are not imposing on others—by panhandling, for instance, which has been known to occur. The appropriate response, therefore, is to have an objective set of admission standards, followed by prompt and even-handed enforcement of rules that all campers are required to follow.

At the front end, for example, some campgrounds ban all RVs more than ten years old, with exceptions possible in some cases after visual inspection by the owner. It's a silly rule, in that there are any number of vintage RVs that have been lovingly restored by their owners, and there's nothing magical about ten years. But at least the rule will screen out most clunkers, and it has the heft of an apparently objective hard-and-fast standard that allows a desk clerk to take refuge behind the phrase, "I'm sorry, but that's the rule." You'll have to decide for yourself whether it's one you want to embrace.

More useful, perhaps, are rules that limit particular kinds of campers to no more than a week on the premises. Pop-ups and tents, for example, are eminently habitable for a few days, but they don't have a lot of floor space, and after a while their occupants inevitably start overflowing their site. The result will be a trashy look that your other campers will find offensive—and so will you.

Best to limit the damage by requiring everyone to pack up and move off the property after five or seven days, pleas and protests notwithstanding, providing of course that you made the time limit crystal clear at check-in.

Meanwhile, at the other end of the rate spectrum, prolonged cabin stays also can become a problem. Unlike a hotel, campgrounds do not provide daily maid service; and while a campground cabin is larger than a tent or pop-up, it's probably still smaller than most hotel rooms and often includes cooking facilities as well. The combination of all these factors, you'll quickly discover, will in most cases create a housekeeping nightmare for your cleaning staff that only gets worse the longer it goes on. A week is probably the most you should allow in cabins, too.

(On the flip side, you might also—depending on customer demand and your staffing levels—consider having a two-day minimum for any lodging stays. Flipping cabins every day within a narrow three- or four-hour window can be more taxing than it's worth if you're short-handed.)

Who do you want as your customer base?

Moving on from issues of short-term vs. long-term campers, a more basic question you'll need to answer is what kind of campers you want overall. Although your customers will come in all shapes, colors and sizes, your policies, amenities, and general vibe will tend to attract more of one kind of camper than another, a process that will reinforce itself through word-of-mouth.

If you belong to one of the two franchise systems, your customer base is already pretty much defined. Jellystone is the ultimate kid-friendly system, while KOA has segmented its brand into three groupings, labeled "Resort," "Holiday" and "Journey," that attempt to define each campground within its network more narrowly. RVers who hold memberships in each system have made a conscious choice about the kind of campground they find most appealing, but even non-members have a pretty clear idea of what to expect from either franchise, thanks to their extensive marketing.

But what if your campground is one of the 9,000 or more independent RV parks that are not part of a franchise or a corporate or investment group portfolio? How will you define yourself?

One way is through explicit, advertised policies that purposefully limit your customer base so that those who camp with you do so in a comfortable, accepting environment. The most extreme example of this is a nudist or clothing-optional campground, where campers may find uni-sex bathrooms and showers, desk staff may be unclothed, and the swimming pool may be surrounded by naked sun-bathers. The people seeking out such a campground don't want to be gawked at, just as people with modesty and body issues don't want to be embarrassed by their reluctance to conform to expectations.

But there are more mainstream subcultures you may want to attract. Some campgrounds, for instance, let it be known that they welcome motorcyclists, others that they're LGBTQ-friendly, by advertising in publications and social media that target those groups. You may want to encourage big rigs—assuming your campground is appropriately laid out—or RVing clubs looking for campgrounds with group facilities, and there are advertising avenues to reach them, as well. On the flip side, you may want to deter some kinds of campers, like the KOA franchisee who recently left the system—and promptly converted her campground to a "55-and-older" property so she no longer has to deal with kids.

If your campground has a large, enclosed dog park and numerous doggie waste containers dispersed on the grounds, you'll attract a certain crowd—and if you want to further encourage its patronage, you might want to think about adding a dog-washing station, or providing a dog-sitting service for campers who want to be free to explore the local area. If you have fast and rock-solid internet access, you can advertise that heavily to the Millennials and Gen-Xers who have taken to working from the road. If your grounds are extensive enough and you can separate some sites from the rest, you might think about creating—and advertising—a no-campfire section, for the increasingly vocal subset of campers who object to woodsmoke for health or aesthetic reasons.

There are, in other words, numerous attributes you can emphasize that will create one kind of campground ambience or another—but as that last example should underscore, some choices will preclude others, so choose wisely.

Unenforced rules and policies less than worthless

Whatever you decide about the kind of campground personality you want to establish, there are two additional factors to keep in mind: consistency, and what I think of as "mission creep."

Consistency is hard. Consistency is your willingness to enforce the rules and policies you've established despite an unremitting assault on them by RVers who want a special exception, or a "favor," or your recognition of why they really, really deserve or need you to bend the rules—just this once! Consistency means engaging in the distasteful and often stomach-churning task of telling people the one thing they least want to hear, which is "No." Consistency is wearing, and it is wearying, and you can tell which campground owners were not up to it in the long run because those RV parks are visibly sliding into anarchic disrepair.

That isn't to say that if your campers are consistently disregarding a particular rule or policy, you shouldn't ask yourself why that is. Some rules are dumb, and some policies are poorly thought-out, and reexamining why they are that way is never inappropriate. But if there is a readily understandable reason for a contested rule or policy, you will do yourself more damage in the long run by not enforcing it than in not having it at all. It's analogous to the "broken windows" theory of policing, in which tolerance for relatively minor infractions encourages more of the same and ultimately feeds a downward spiral of bad behavior. And while you may not have bought a campground with the idea that you were taking on a policeman's role, this indeed is just one of the many hats you'll be wearing.

Along those lines, it's further worth noting that your campers, however narrowly you may try to define them as a group, nonetheless will encompass the entire range of human personalities. The great majority will be absolutely swell people, looking to please you and to understand and follow your expectations because they're not camping with you to get into squabbles—they're simply out to have a good time, and the more clearly defined your boundaries, the more comfortable they'll be. But you'll also have to contend with some number of campers with anger issues, campers who are self-absorbed and oblivious to their surroundings, campers who feel entitled and demanding of everyone they encounter.

That's all part and parcel of being in the "hospitality" business, which one wag defined as "making your customers feel like they're at home even when you wish they were." You may find this to be the hardest part of this enterprise you've undertaken, and one that isn't mentioned much (if at all) by those who promote campground ownership. It can lead to burnout, it stresses marriages and family life, and ultimately explains why so many mom-and-pop campgrounds are put up for sale within the first decade of ownership.

The other tendency I want to caution you about is "mission creep," the pressure you'll feel from all sides to constantly expand, enhance and "modernize" what you're offering. You may recall, near the beginning of this book, how I warned you about the opportunists pitching all kinds of over-priced books, recordings, courses and seminars to potential campground buyers. Although some of what they offer may be worthwhile, they're essentially preying on the anxiety and self-doubt that afflict most people when they're plunging into uncharted waters. It's only natural to want help and reassurance when undertaking something new, and that's as true now that you own a campground as it was when you were looking to buy one—there's just a new cast of characters involved.

You will discover, for example, that if you attend industry workshops or conventions, virtually every session will be led by someone who's actually trying to sell you a product or service. Whatever the problem with which you're wrestling—how to improve campground wi-fi, for instance—the person leading the session almost invariably will be a representative for one of the major campground wi-fi vendors. Whatever the latest trend may be—glamping, as another example—workshops on the subject will be led by teepee or Conestoga wagon or yurt manufacturers, and trade shows will be replete with all these and related products, offered at a convention discount to goose sales.

Beware of mouse envy

Yet underlying all these self-serving spiels is an even more pernicious sales pitch, and that's for a highly commercialized version of hospitality most closely identified with the Walt Disney amusement park empire. Why "pernicious"? Because it incorporates several unacknowledged assumptions, starting with the premise that camping should be a curated activity shaped by the campground operator; and because it gains its authority through association with the Disney brand—which most campground owners, after even a moment's reflection, should realize is like drawing comparisons between operating a food truck and managing a high-end chain of restaurants. They both serve food, but. . . .

Differences in scale, financial resources, price points, clientele, and customer expectations notwithstanding, a cottage industry of speakers and consultants will make every effort to convince you that it's your job to transform the humdrum business of camping into something "magical." They'll point to Disney's growth rate, to the astronomical sums it earns each year and to its high-flying customer ratings, and they'll ask you why you wouldn't like to do something similar. And in years past, they would distill Disney's success to one basic formula that anyone—presumably—could emulate: it was all about customer service.

But that was then, and this is now—and customer service is so yesterday. "Providing customer service is not good enough—

customer service is a waste of time," a former Disney executive who is now busy as a consultant told campground owners at the 2021 ARVC convention. Instead, "customer experience is the next competitive battleground" —and by "customer experience" he meant an emphasis on the new and unexpected, on the "wow" factor embodied in amenities such as zip lines, lazy rivers and climbing walls, or in exotic lodging like treehouses.

Emphasizing the "wow"' factor—get used to hearing that a lot—isn't inherently a bad thing, but it certainly is a defining choice for a campground and the kind of campers it will attract, and therefore deserving of careful evaluation. Moreover, it will put you on a slippery slope, because an essential component of "wow" is constant innovation—as witness any Disney park— which means constant reinvestment in new amenities and additional staffing, not to mention higher costs for your campers. You might, in fact, decide that is exactly the kind of campground you want to operate, and in that case more power to you. But arrive at that decision deliberately and after looking at it from all sides, not because you got stampeded into it by a fast-talking consultant or by industry peer pressure.

And keep in mind that with campgrounds, as in life generally, every choice you make precludes other options—that opening one door usually means closing others. If your ideal campground is a modest affair with just a few dozen sites, basic hookups, a bathhouse and laundry and a lot of trees but little else, keeping your eye on the ball will be a lot easier than if you own something bigger, more complex and less focused.   ✑

Chapter 9:
Who Pays What, and How Much?

ONE OF THE MORE CONFOUNDING aspects of running a campground is figuring out how to manage the revenue side of things. Although some of your income will come from store sales, and some from activities fees (if any), the lion's share will be derived from what you charge your guests to camp on your property. That includes site fees, of course, but also a bunch of associated charges that you may or may not wish to levy: site-lock fees, cancellation fees, holiday premium rates, extra fees for making reservations either on the phone or online, early-arrival or late-departure fees, additional camper fees, extra vehicle fees, and on and on. On the flip side, there's also the question of whether you should offer discounts or have discounted rates for longer stays, or perhaps offer some kind of frequent-customer reward.

Further muddying the waters is the accelerating move toward "dynamic" or "demand" pricing, which is the model used most prominently by the airline industry but which also has become standard at hotels and across the accommodations industry in general. The approach does away with the fixed prices that were the industry standard until recently, replacing them with algorithm-driven rates that change from day-to-day and even hour-to-hour, depending on your supply of sites and customer demand for them. As with airline reservations, if you book well ahead of time, the cost of a site will tend to be lower than if you wait, rewarding those who plan ahead. Prices will then rise as a particular date draws closer, but if a site still hasn't been reserved a day or two out, will drop significantly—rewarding those who were willing to gamble the site wouldn't be booked out from under them.

This lack of pricing transparency can be enormously frustrating for campers who simply want to know the cost of things. Until a couple of years ago they could still get an answer to the question, "What's it cost to stay at your campground?" even in the absence of one universal price: weekends would cost more than weekdays, summers were more expensive than off-season, pull-throughs were pricier than back-ins, full hook-ups cost more than water and electric sites, and on and on. For all that, however, Site X would cost Y Dollars on Date Z, and that wouldn't change until the next year, if then. If an RVer wanted to know what it would cost to stay at your park, you could give him a rate sheet spelling out all the possibilities in black and white. Now you're essentially limited to responding with, "Our full hook-up sites start at X."

You could still do things the old-fashioned way, of course—but as noted, the trend overall is toward the dynamic model. This development has been accelerated by a crowded online-reservation industry, which at this writing is in a furious competitive battle for market share that stresses all the ways it can improve your bottom line. Dynamic pricing, which prior to computerized reservations systems would have been inconceivable, is one way. Another is the institutionalization of site-lock fees, which enable a camper—for a price—to reserve not just "a" site, but a specific site; not just a 50-amp full hook-up pull-through near the lake, but site 17 specifically. Many campground managers previously avoided making those ironclad arrangements because it limited their flexibility to maximize site utilization, but the algorithms take care of that, too, shifting around reservations that aren't locked in to ensure as many sites as possible are always occupied.

Regardless of whether you adopt dynamic pricing and site-lock fees, however, it still will be up to you to determine your base rates. You've bought a campground that has an existing fee structure: is it what you want? Should your rates be increased—or even, in some cases, reduced?

Analyze your occupancy rates

An obvious first step toward answering that question, as mentioned in Chapter 6, is to look at the competition. If nearby campgrounds of comparable quality and with similar amenities are charging a lot more than you are, that may be a clue that you can raise your rates as well. But if there are no comparable competitors, or if there are but their rates are not appreciably different from yours, you still should look at your internal data to see how rate adjustments might better balance your occupancy load.

For example, if your pull-though sites are at or near full occupancy in certain time periods but your equivalent (same utilities) back-ins are at 50% occupancy, raising the rates on the pull-throughs may push some of those reservations toward the underutilized back-in sites. That not only will increase utilization of the back-ins, but may attract campers who must have a pull-through but weren't able to find an acceptable site previously, re-sulting in an overall increase of reservations across both kinds of sites despite the increased rate.

The same logic applies to full hook-up sites vs. just water and electric, or 50-amp sites vs. 30 amps. Sites with more or higher-level amenities should charge more, but if they're not priced high enough, they'll be booked by RVers who actually could do with less, making their supply scarcer. Few reservations will be as frustrating for you as the pop-up trailer on a full hookup, 50-amp pull-through site when your campground is packed to the gills. If you see that hap-pening, bump the base rate accordingly.

Aside from balancing occupancy across your various site types, you also should be paying attention to overall occupancy. Although it might seem counter-intuitive, you do not want 100% occupancy—even 90% occupancy on a consistent basis is too high—because it means you're not charging enough. Once you hit that high an occupancy, you don't know how many campers got turned away because there were no spaces left, which is income you've missed out on. Or as a CPA who specializes in campground accounting put it, "When occupancy rates start hitting 75% or 80%, it's time to raise prices."

Raising rates will drive down occupancy, which means less stress on the facilities and on staff, and if balanced correctly will bring in just as much (if not more) income as before. Over time the occupancy rate will start inching up again, because of continued high demand and waning price resistance, and eventually you'll be able to raise the rates again. Meanwhile, the CPA I just quoted also believes that campgrounds need to do away with weekly and monthly rates, at least in season, when the potential to fill those sites at overnight rates means "you're just giving money away" with a discount.

Indeed, there's an argument to be made for doing away with all discounts, which tend to cheapen the product. That flies in the face of contemporary expectations, since most RVers are so used to getting a discount of one kind or another that not having one offered can be a slap in the face—reason enough for you to tread cautiously here. Indeed, some campground owners build a discount into their prices just so they can make campers feel like they're getting a "deal," hollow though it may be. The possibilities are so numerous that it's a rare camper who doesn't qualify for one: KOA and Good Sam both have 10% discounts at participating campgrounds, but there also are savings to be had for being in the military (retired or active) or a first responder, for being an AAA member, for being a member of Passport America, the Escapees RV Club or the Family Motor Coach Association, (again, at participating campgrounds), even just for being old.

Other charges you should consider

Aside from basic site rates, campgrounds can have a smorgasbord of other fees that they charge, only some of which were mentioned at the start of this chapter. This is a fraught subject for many campground owners, because while some fees exist to deter certain kinds of behavior, most are an attempt to recoup real costs. The customer-relations problem this can create for you is when there are so many fees that campers start feeling they're being nickeled-and-dimed to death, giving rise to gibes like the claim that KOA actually means "Keep On Adding."

One response by some campground owners is to dispense with virtually all add-on fees and simply have a high enough base rate to cover their increased costs. Yet because this approach can result in sticker shock, one not-infrequent response is a demand by campers for *a la carte* pricing: why, they'll ask, should we pay for wi-fi we're not using, or for access to a swimming pool we have no intention of patronizing? There's no easy resolution of these conflicting demands, so whichever route you take, be assured there'll be some complaints.

Here are some campground fees you should consider:

Cancellation fees: Once upon a time, campers could make a reservation and if their plans changed, cancel them at little or no cost. No more. Demand for sites is so high that a cancelled reservation means the loss of assured income, with only a reduced chance that it might be replaced. Most campgrounds therefore require at least one night's advance payment to hold a site, with an increasing number moving to require full payment either when the reservation is made, or a week or more before arrival. Cancelling a reservation may mean forfeiture of all money paid by that date, or only a partial refund that gets smaller the longer a camper waits to cancel. Even the most generous cancellation policy will include some kind of handling charge, of at least $10 but possibly quite a bit more, to cover staff time and credit card fees.

Cancellation fees are one of the most contentious areas with which you may end up dealing. Most RVers will shrug off their losses, but some will go down kicking and screaming over the equivalent of a couple of cups of Starbucks coffee. They'll cite extenuating circumstances, challenging you to reject claims of a family death, equipment breakdown or a search for a runaway pet. They'll point out that you'll make the money back by renting the site to someone else—which may or may not turn out to be true, but which in any case shifts the risk to you. Ultimately, they'll dispute the charge with their credit card issuer, causing you either to contest the chargeback or to eat the loss so you don't waste a lot of time on the required documentation.

You'll have to decide for yourself how much of this you can tolerate, but don't make the mistake of thinking you can avoid it altogether by getting rid of cancellation fees—the no-shows will eat you alive. On the other hand, whatever policy you come up with, make sure it's fully communicated to campers, in writing, before they make a reservation and again after they've paid their deposit. You'll need that documentation down the road.

Extra campers/extra vehicle fees: Most, if not all, campgrounds specify that their rates are for a set number of campers and a maximum number of vehicles, for self-evident reasons. The number of campers covered by the site fee usually is either two or four, with an additional charge per head ranging between $2 and $10, and possibly higher at campgrounds with a lot of amenities bundled into the site fee. Historically, campgrounds had different rates for adults and kids, but that distinction has been disappearing in the wake of arguments about who is and is not a "kid." Different campgrounds set the cut-off age at 5, 12 or 17, and then had to defend not only their choice, but why someone who just turned 13 last week should be charged a higher rate than he was a month earlier. It's much less trouble to just count all heads the same.

A related issue is whether you'll want to set a maximum number of people per site, regardless of how the site fee is structured. Your campground has finite resources, and every additional person on the grounds adds to the septic load, the swimming pool occupancy and the amount of hot water running through your showers, so you have an obvious interest in moderating the population impact. One way to do that is by capping site occupancy, typically at six, which usually is more than enough—but there are a surprising number of families that include two parents and six children, with perhaps a grandmother thrown in to help ride herd on the kids. You should take these incidents on a case-by-case basis, making exceptions when circumstances allow and consoling yourself with the thought that many other sites are occupied by only two or three people.

Potentially more problematic is the proliferation of personal vehicles at many campgrounds, as campers rendezvous at the park instead of traveling together. This can result in your sites looking more like parking lots than camping spots, while also adding to the overall amount of vehicular traffic on the property. One response, provided you have adequate alternatives, is to have a limit of only one vehicle—in addition to the RV—allowed on each site, with excess vehicles consigned to a visitor parking area. A supplemental approach is to charge $10 a day for parking for each additional vehicle, mostly as a way of discouraging the practice.

Guest fees: Closely related to fees for extra campers are fees for guests who are visiting campers, and for similar reasons: additional bodies mean additional demands on your amenities and infrastructure. Yet you can't reasonably prohibit your guests from entertaining their own guests, frequently including relatives or friends who live in the area. So what do you do?

Some campgrounds, reasoning that the problem of too many guests on the property is too rare to get worked up about, don't charge anything extra—although even in that case, it's prudent to require guests of guests to register at the office so you have some idea of who's on the premises. Others will have a nominal fee—perhaps $5 a head—and still others have a nominal fee that gets refunded if the guest stay for only a limited time, such as a couple of hours. The refundable fee accommodates someone coming for dinner with one of your campers, while still bringing in income from those who want to use your facilities for a day of fun in the sun.

Reservation fees: Once a rarity, reservation fees—fees campers are charged for the privilege of spending their money for a reservation—are showing up more frequently as a way of channeling traffic. Initially, these fees were an add-on for campers making online reservations, to defray the costs charged by the outside service providers, and could be avoided simply by picking up a phone. More recently, however, this logic has been flipped on its head, with no extra charge for online reservations—the campground eats those costs—but with a "convenience fee" (or some such euphemism) tacked on for those making a telephone reservation. The economic logic behind this move is that it enables the campground to operate with shorter office hours and a smaller desk staff. The downside, which you'll have to weigh, is that a business claiming to be in the hospitality industry is forsaking the personal touch that is at the very core of hospitality—a trend further exacerbated by the increased reliance on "remote check-ins."

There is one other "benefit" to you for pushing customers toward online reservations: campers who prefer to use the phone rather than go online trend older, and they're more inclined to complain about prices.

Early arrival/late departure fees: As with every other rule and guideline you may adopt, there always will be those seeking an exception to the arrival and departure times you set. If you don't ban these exceptions outright, you can at least make the transgressors pay for the inconvenience they're causing.

Most campgrounds set a check-out time of 11 a.m., noon or 1 p.m., with a check-in time that might be as early as noon but usually starts at 1 or 2 p.m. (Check-in times for cabins are usually later, starting at 3 or 4 p.m., to give the housekeeping staff enough time to clean up after departures.) The interval gives your maintenance crew enough time to pick up litter, clean out fire pits and do any other required maintenance, such a raking gravel sites, before the next campers arrive. Yet despite the obvious logic of having arrivals come only after departures have, well, departed, you will have RVers rolling in at 8 or 9 or 10 in the morning, fully expecting to be able to occupy a site and becoming quite indignant if told otherwise.

You may or may not have a site open that meets their requirements, but there's at least some chance that if someone occupied it the previous night, it hasn't been cleaned yet—and if the arriving camper had locked in a specific site, there's an even smaller chance that it will be available at that hour. If you can't accommodate the early bird, his or her choice is to leave and come back later or to sit in a parking area—assuming you have the space. On the other hand, if an appropriate site is available, you might consider charging an early arrival fee, typically between $10 and $20. (Some campgrounds, you should note, charge by the hour for early arrivals.) As with the extra vehicle fee, this charge is designed more to discourage such behavior than as a profit center.

On the other end, there are campers who either blatantly or inadvertently disregard your check-out time, or who come into the office the morning of their scheduled departure and ask if they can stay extra hours. Charge them all—if the site they're in hasn't been reserved for someone arriving that afternoon. Otherwise, you'll have to start breathing down their necks to get them out of there.

Dumping fees: If your campground has a dump station—and it should—for RVers wishing to empty their black waste tanks, you are likely to get calls from travelers through the area asking if they can use it, too. Your registered campers should be able to use the dump station without an extra charge, and some campgrounds will extend a similar courtesy to passing travelers. On the other hand, accepting people's sewage incurs a cost for you, whether from a local municipality that treats your waste or from the septic service that periodically pumps out your sludge tanks. Many campgrounds, therefore, will charge non-campers a modest dumping fee, typically between $10 and $25.

In addition to the dump station, many campgrounds—especially if they have a significant number of non-sewered sites—operate a portable pump-out tank euphemistically referred to as a "honey wagon." Honey wagon visits typically are reserved by campers unable or unwilling to use your dump station, and in most cases also carry a charge between $10 and $25 per pump-out. A honey wagon also can be used as an inducement for campers to reserve non-sewered sites that are under-utilized, with an offer of a free pump-out every two to three nights for those particular spots.

Activities fees: Many campgrounds don't have any activity fees—usually because they don't have much in the way of activities. Others, however, may offer a full menu, ranging from various arts and crafts to organized activities to laser tag, rock-wall climbing, mini- or disc-golf, bike and boat rentals, bouncing pillows, splash pads, water slides and even paintball tournaments. One way to pay for all that is through activity-specific fees, but for families with several kids that can mount up pretty quickly, so some campgrounds sell activity bracelets that for one price offer access to all the exrra amenities. You can do something similar. A third approach is to cover the cost of some activities in the base rate, leaving others as add-ons. Which approach works best for you will depend on what you have—there's no rule of thumb for this.

Pet fees: Most campgrounds accept pets without any extra charge, with one exception: if they have pet-friendly lodging, that usually comes with a nightly per-pet fee, typically around $5. The fee covers additional cleaning costs—like vacuuming pet hair off the furniture—and is in addition to a refundable pet deposit that is intended to compensate for any damage a pet may cause. Note: such fees may not be charged legally for service animals, which are not considered "pets."

Wi-fi fees: Forget 'em. Some campgrounds still have these, as a carryover from a time when wi-fi was considered a luxury amenity, but these days internet access is as essential as water and electricity. If you have such fees, all they'll do is aggravate your campers—and even more so if your wi-fi service is not up to snuff.

The thorny subject of refunds

Any discussion of "who pays for what" isn't complete without a look at that least attractive of all transactions, the refund.

Unlike hard goods, like digital TVs or canned goods, your product is ephemeral—once a date has come and gone, that reservation can never be resold. If you're a car dealer and have a customer who orders a brand-new vehicle but then changes his mind before taking delivery, well, you've still got a brand-new car you can sell. If you own a campground and one of your campers has a site reserved for today but doesn't show up, that time-dependent product can't be resold. It's no different than if you buy a concert ticket but miss the show: that seat for that date has slipped into the past, regardless of whether your butt was planted in it or not.

As obvious as that might seem to you as a campground owner, it's not always as obvious to your campers. From their perspective, they paid for something that they're not getting, and they can get mighty righteous about demanding they get their money back. An unexpected death back home, a suddenly sick spouse, a highway accident—any number of uncontrollable events may have prevented a camper from keeping his side of the deal he'd made with you, which was that he'd give you money in exchange for a guarantee that you'd hold a site for him. But since it wasn't his fault that he couldn't keep up his end of the bargain, you'd have to be a real skinflint not to return his deposit—or at least that's how some campers will view matters.

But aside from the not uncommon possibility that your camper is making it all up—that he'd double- or triple-booked a reservation at several campgrounds to give himself options, or that he'd simply changed his plans at the last moment—the demand for a refund is your camper's attempt to off-load on you the risks he'd accepted when making his plans. Why he was unable to keep his reservation should be no more relevant to you than your reasons for not having the site he'd reserved would be relevant to him. If a local power outage meant you couldn't provide your sites with water and electricity, or if you had a flood and parts of the camp-ground were unexpectedly inaccessible, or . . . whatever the reason, if you can't provide a camper with a reserved site, it's on you. You're the one who, when taking his deposit, accepted a risk that for one reason or another you might not have that site available for the date it was booked.

These aren't merely academic musings. When the pan-demic struck in March 2020, campgrounds throughout the United States were shut down almost overnight. Most campground own-ers had little if any clue as to when they'd be allowed to reopen, and so were faced with the enormous task of contacting scores, if not hundreds, of campers who had booked sites for the com-ing months to let them know their reservations had to be can-celled. Some, naturally, wanted their deposits refunded. Others were willing to transfer their deposits to new reservations, made for later that summer, in the hope that the campground would be reopened by then. Still others were offered a deal of one kind or another, such as allowing the campground to keep the deposit in excahnge for applying it toward a 50% discount for any reserva-tion made in the next year.

Regardless of how the debt was settled, the costs of pan-demic closures clearly had to be borne by campground owners, not their customers. It follows, therefore, that when the shoe is on the other foot, it is the customer who is on the hook. You have to keep that truth firmly in mind and be prepared to patiently explain it to an irate customer, or risk getting steamrollered.

That said, you also need to remember that this is a people business. You are in the hospitality industry, and being hospitable may mean—in some cases—that it's only humane to give a full or partial refund, or to offer a rain check, for a clearly distraught camper who is not just being manipulative. It's your call. That's called good customer relations—as long as it's not the result of being browbeaten.

There is one other refund situation particular to the camp-ground industry that needs mention. Camping is, by definition, an activity that involves interacting with nature—and nature isn't always pleasant. Unlike stadium events that might be called on account of rain, camping entails dealing with excessive heat or cold, thunderstorms and possible flooding, high winds or snow. Unless the weather is so extreme that it threatens life or limb, that's part of the package that comes with a campground reservation and there should be no refunds for rain—or, as you'll sometimes encounter, even the possibility of rain. You're in no position to make any promises about the weather, nor should you bear the costs if the weather is not to someone's liking.

Campers always have the option of packing up and going home early if they're not having a good time, but that's their choice. As we would tell campers who would ask about weather-related refunds, "We don't charge extra for the sunshine, and we don't give refunds for the rain." ✌

Chapter 10:
Other Things You Need to Know

WHILE THE PRECEDING NINE chapters have covered most of what you need to know to get into the campground business, there are a few other things worth thinking about, starting with cabins.

If you've bought a Jellystone or KOA, it's a given that you already have cabins, and quite possibly a lot of them. Jellystone's primary market is families, not RVers, so while its franchisees certainly have a lot of RV sites, the company appeals to as broad a swath of its target audience as possible by heavily promoting cabin rentals to the non-RVing public. KOA, meanwhile, has positioned itself as offering camping opportunities whatever your personal preference, be it in an RV, a tent, a cabin or any of a variety of glamping possibilities. Even most KOA Journeys, which are at the no-frills end of the KOA spectrum, have basic cabins, while KOA Holidays and KOA Resorts offer deluxe cabins that include bathrooms and kitchenettes.

So does that mean, even if you're not a Jellystone or KOA, that your campground should have cabins, too? In a word, no.

If you already have cabins, fine. But if you don't, or if you think you want more, you need to think about a couple of things. The first is that unless you're going to put new cabins in an area that is currently undeveloped, you'll almost certainly put them in existing RV sites. That's the easiest and fastest route to take, since a deluxe cabin has the same water, electric and sewer requirements as a large RV, and in some cases this will be a smart way to repurpose a problem site—for example, sites with low occupancy levels because they're hard to back into. Or sites that are not level and would be difficult to rework, but which can accommodate a cabin on pilings.

But replacing full hook-up RV sites, which are in high demand, with cabins that may not be quite as sought after, requires a careful cost-benefit analysis. If your existing cabins are heavily booked, that might suggest there's enough demand to justify expanding inventory—but it also may mean you should be charging higher rates. If you decide nonetheless to add a cabin, you'll need to balance costs against anticipated revenues, both for the existing RV site and for its replacement; compare the two to see how long it will take for the change to be profitable—to calculate your return on investment, or ROI, as the money boys like to put it. You may find the results discouraging.

Consider that a new deluxe cabin starts at around $30,000 for the cheapest 300-square-foot models, but can easily be twice that. This bseline cost is the figure cabin proponents like to tout, noting that if you charge $100 a night and rent out the cabin for just 100 nights a year—which you may or may not accomplish—then you'll get your money back in just three years. Rent it out for 150 nights and your ROI is just two years!

But there's more to a cabin's costs than its sticker price. You'll have to add shipping, set-up and skirting costs; construction of a requisite deck or patio; and interior furnishings, including furniture, dishes, cookware and a flat-panel TV. Then there are ongoing costs, such as insurance, taxes, and licenses, which vary by jurisdiction. And don't forget to factor in the cost of linens, laundry, and cleaning supplies, as well as the cost of replacing trashed or stolen equipment—all expenses that RV owners incur for themselves, but which you'll now be absorbing. And, of course, if you're not repurposing an existing RV site, there's the added expense of creating a new pad and utility hookups. In short, a two- or three-year ROI turns out to be a pipe dream.

There is yet one more variable that you have to throw into the mix, and that's the added manpower that cabins demand:

someone has to clean them, at a time when housekeeping staff has become extremely hard to recruit. And someone has to do the ongoing maintenance that all buildings require, from restaining wood siding to replacing roofs to guarding against mold, mildew and pest infestation. These, also, are costs you don't have when renting to RVers.

Speaking of pests . . .

Pest control is an expense you'll already have factored into your overall budgeting, because even without cabins you still have structures that need protection from rodents, termites, carpenter bees, wasps and other infestations. But there's one pest that's pretty much unique to cabins, and that you're bound to encounter sooner or later: bed bugs.

The bane of all accommodation providers, bed bugs are a pest that are introduced by your guests themselves. Unlike all those other pests that your exterminator protects against, bed bugs don't come in from the great outdoors through gaps in floorboards or siding, or by hitching a ride on a mouse—they arrive tucked into the sheets or sleeping bags of your campers, who may have picked them up at another campground or in their own homes. For that reason, some campgrounds provide linens in all their cabins and discourage campers from bringing their own, albeit with questionable effectiveness, since guests arriving from a bed bug environment can just as easily transport them in their luggage. Still, you might give that approach a whirl.

Once you do get bed bugs, you'll learn about it from subsequent campers who rent the infested cabin. There's really nothing much you can do for your bitten customers, other than offer a refund and have them use your laundry machines to eliminate any bugs from their personal possessions before they return home. But you will need to close the affected cabin until it's been treated, and in my experience, the only truly effective remediation is to hire a heat treatment specialist, who will seal off the entire structure and bake it at 120 to 140 degrees for several hours. Heat treatment is expensive—figure on spending at least $1,000 per cabin—but because it penetrates cracks and gets into walls where bed bugs may be hiding, and also kills any eggs, it's significantly more effective than pesticide sprays or bombs. Less toxic to humans, too.

Smoking and pets

Two more common aggravations you may face with cabin rentals is smoking and pets—assuming, that is, that you have cabins that prohibit one or the other. Smoking is all but universally banned in public accommodations, and most campgrounds will permit pets only in some (if any) rental units, so that customers with pet dander allergies aren't adversely affected. Despite your rules, however—and without regard for even the most conspicuous signage—you'll have campers who will smuggle dogs into pet-free cabins or who think they'll escape notice if they smoke beside an open window.

Your recourse, in these circumstances, is to have clearly articulated policies that state the financial consequences of breaking your rules, and to require a deposit of at least $100 from anyone renting your cabins. Since in most cases you won't learn the rules have been broken until after the campers have checked out, you should document whatever evidence you can find—and resign yourself to the inevitability of some transgressions being unprovable. You won't be able to record the smell of cigarette smoke—even though you'll need to air out the cabin before it's re-rented, and possibly run an ozone generator as well—but you might find cigarette stains, cigarette ash or even dishes that clearly were used as ashtrays. Photograph everything. Ditto for dog hair, claw marks or other evidence of pets brought into non-pet cabins.

Then keep the deposit and send your departed camper a note to that effect, and be prepared to submit your documentation to a credit card issuer when the camper squawks.

Campground safety

Like it or not, as the owner of a public facility you share responsibility for the physical safety of your campers. Some of that boils down to obvious measures, such as removing trip hazards, spraying for stinging insects in playground areas, putting fire extinguishers in cabins and laundry rooms, and enforcing the park's speed limits. Some of it may be dictated by local or state regulations, which can vary considerably from one jurisdiction to another: for example, some states require lifeguards at swimming pools while others do not, providing there are prominent signs posted to that effect. And some things you could be doing may not be immediately obvious, or may not be legally required, but which upon even a moment's reflection become a no-brainer.

One example of this last point is having automatic external defibrillators publicly accessible at key locations around the campground. AEDs these days are commonly distributed in airport terminals, recreational facilities and hotels, but are surprisingly rare in campgrounds—which, when you think about it, have a significant percentage of customers with the highest probability of needing one. They're not cheap—figure on spending at least $1,000 per unit—and may seem like an unnecessary expense, given how rarely they're used, but you only have to use an AED once to realize it was money well spent.

Because AEDs are considered almost idiot-proof and can be applied successfully by someone without prior training, simply having them mounted in visible locations would be a huge step forward—but hands-on exposure to your staff is even better, especially if it's combined with CPR (cardiopulmonary resuscitation) training. Courses are widely provided by the American Red Cross and other agencies, last half-a-day and are nominally priced. Run your inside and outside staffs through a session once a year and you've just made your RV park an immeasurably safer place for staff and campers alike.

A broader question you should consider is how your staff

will respond to an emergency. That's not a subject you'll run across at a campground owners' convention, but having a crisis-response plan that's understood by your staff is at least as important as any other training you may provide, and can mean a critical difference in outcomes. Such plans should include a description of who is to respond to the scene of an emergency, and with what equipment; who is to notify emergency responders; and who is to record essential information about the emergency. This information should be provided to first-responders as they arrive, but as critically, should become part of a case file maintained by the campground for your insurance company and, in case of litigation, your lawyers.

You also may find it prudent to devise an emergency alert and evacuation plan for your campers. This obviously is most called for in areas frequently battered by tornadoes, where a growing number of campgrounds are equipped with bunkers or other shelters, but not all your campers will know where they're located—or even when they should take refuge. Other campgrounds may be vulnerable to flooding or forest fires, and even the most environmentally secure RV park can be threatened by a man-made catastrophe, such as a leaking RV propane tank, that may prompt a local fire department to order an evacuation. The more you think this through ahead of an actual catastrophe and plan your contingent responses, the better your chances of keeping a potential disaster from becoming an actual one.

Finally, it's a useful exercise to look at your campground through a first-responder's eyes. Depending on your park's size and topography, an ambulance or fire engine driver might find it confusing to navigate in daylight, much less at night while pumped up on adrenaline. Reach out to your local fire chief or ambulance squad president for a walk-through to find out what they think would help them in an emergency, such as a couple of dry-runs during your slow season. Provide them with site maps and your cell-phone number or other contact information. One arrangement we established at our park was to have the 911 operator call us, immediately after dispatching first-responders, to let us know what kind of emergency had been called in and where. That enabled us to give assistance as needed before first-responders could arrive, as well as be ready to provide them with an escort directly to the scene.

One thing that you might want to track is a limited but growing state-by-state initiative to enact legislation giving campgrounds liability protection from frivolous lawsuits. Usually described as "inherent risks of camping" legislation, the laws protect prudent campground owners from lawsuits over risks that are beyond their control, such as tripping over a tree root, getting burnt by a campfire or being hit by lightning. Wisconsin was the first state to adopt such legislation, Ohio and Missouri followed suit, and at least half-a-dozen others are in various stages of considering it.

Electric vehicles

It was only a few years ago that campground wi-fi was an add-on, a nice-to-have but not critical amenity that might be available only in a small part of an RV park. Today it's often a make-or-break utility, as critical to many campers' decision-making about where they'll camp as the availability of 50-amp hookups. And today, charging capacity for electric vehicles is at the same stage of development.

In addition to Ford's F150 Lightning and GM's electric Silverado and Hummer, all capable of towing trailers and fifth-wheels, manufacturers are starting to produce towable RVs that have electric motors powering their wheels, extending the range of their tow vehicles. And the one thing all these battery-powered motors will need when they reach a campground is a way to recharge their systems, preferably overnight, preferably while camped in one of your sites. That means that you should be figuring out which of your sites can be adapted most readily to provide 240-volt level 2 charging power, as well as where you can best place stand-alone recharging stations for those arriving in Teslas, Leafs, Bolts and other more conventional electric vehicles.

If you'll be upgrading pedestals to incorporate EV plug-in features, think also about remote metering of the pedestals so you can charge for electricity without having to dispatch an employee to look at a meter before a camper checks out. This is still cutting-edge technology—but may already be commonplace by the time you read this, because that's how fast everything is changing.

Golf cars

A form of electric vehicle—as well as its gas-powered cousin—already common at many campgrounds is the golf car, owned either by the camper or by you, as a rental amenity. You should think about how you want to regulate these, since they're not toys and can, in fact, cause considerable damage and injury if misused.

Most campgrounds will permit campers to bring their own—sometimes charging an additional fee for the privilege—subject to certain rules, such as requiring all operators to have a regular driver's license or to be a minimum age, requiring front and rear lights for night driving or requiring that they be operated only on established roads. You also should require the owners to provide proof of liability insurance, which most will readily produce; if they can't, have them get their insurance agent to fax or email you a copy. If, on the other hand, you don't want to bother with all that and decide simply to prohibit golf cars from being operated on your property, make sure you advertise the ban boldly and up front to head off as many arguments as possible—one of the problems you'll encounter when most campgrounds permit something that you don't.

Some campgrounds will allow both gas and electric golf cars, while some will permit only the electric variety, which are much quieter. The amount of your electricity these cars will consume to recharge their batteries is negligible, and a good tradeoff for the peace and quiet you'll be gaining. As with a total ban on golf cars, however, if you decide to prohibit the gas-driven variety, make sure you advertise that policy boldly and up-front.

Should you have your own golf cars available as rentals? Those who do say they're a nice profit center, although I didn't find that to be the case at our campground. But regardless, keep in mind that a) they're not cheap; b) they'll require cleaning and maintenance—and repairs if your campers bang them up; and c) they'll add to the overall level of campground traffic, which may already be greater than you or many of your campers find acceptable.

Campfires and firewood

One thing many campers believe is an essential part of the experience is having a campfire. Others—unbelievably!—not so much.

Who doesn't look forward to sitting around a cozy fire as night crawls across the sky, firewood snapping and popping from the heat, skewered marshmallows dripping into the flames as sparks swirl upward? Quite a few people, it turns out, and their numbers may be growing. Some campers object to having their clothes reek of wood smoke, others complain about smoke blowing into their RVs—especially if the sites are unfortunately close to each other—and some are simply allergic to combustion byproducts. Even the most stalwart campfire afficionados may find themselves complaining over a load of inadequately seasoned wood that produces more smoke than fire.

There are some few jurisdictions where this doesn't become a problem in the first place; Las Vegas, for example, doesn't permit open fires within its municipal boundaries, so its campgrounds don't have fire pits. But because those are the exception, you'll have to decide whether campfires are an issue at your property, and if so, whether there's anything you can do about them short of a total ban. One possibility, depending on the size and layout of the campground, is to have a designated no-campfire area. If you decide to go that route, start modestly, market it aggressively—the way other businesses marketed "no smoking" areas before tobacco use began to fade—and see what kind of response you get. If the option proves popular, you can always expand the no-campfire zone more easily than you'll be able to trim one that's too big.

Another approach some campgrounds have started embracing is to do away with individual fire pits in favor of one (or more) large communal rings. These can be quite elaborate, with raised hearths and extensive paving, and can be promoted as evening gathering places for music and conversation among campers who might otherwise never get to interact.

As long as your guests are permitted to have their own campfires, there are two considerations you have to keep in mind. The first is the possibility of local bans on open fires, even in jurisdictions that don't have a standing prohibition, at certain times of the year or under adverse weather conditions. It'll be your responsibility to keep updated on such bans, and it'll be your responsibility to communicate—and enforce—them to your campers. Unfortunately, there will be times when you'll get pushback, sometimes belligerently so.

The other consideration for you to think about is where the firewood your campers will be burning is coming from. Ideally, they'll be buying it from you, and your wood will be locally sourced and properly seasoned, but some campers will insist on bringing their own. If they're buying it from a local supermarket in kiln-dried shrink-wrapped bundles, that's probably not an issue. On the other hand, if there's a loose jumble of logs thrown into the back of a pick-up that drove in from a neighboring state, that could be a huge problem, depending on what kinds of insects have hitchhiked along. State and federal campgrounds across the country prohibit transporting of firewood for that very reason, and you should, too. At our campground, every single ash tree—and there were dozens—was killed within a single season by the emerald ash borer, which almost certainly got imported to our property in a camper's firewood supply.

This isn't an easy prohibition to enforce—are you willing to turn away a camper who just drove 200 miles for a two-night stay? —but the alternative can be grim. You'll get a lot of pushback on this one, too.

Continuing education

Last but not least, there's the question of how you're going to keep up with the times: with changing fashions and expectations among campers, evolving campground technology, new federal or state regulations that affect how you do business and all the other moving pieces of an incredibly dynamic industry.

One obvious place to start is outlined in Chapter 2, in the discussion about how you can start educating yourself about the basics: the National Association of RV Parks and Campgrounds and its state-specific off-shoots, *Woodall's Campground Magazine*, RVtravel, KOA and Jellystone conventions—anywhere, really, where people like you congregate, in person or virtually, to exchange information and ideas. Those resources will be just as useful to you as a campground owner as they were when you were just window shopping.

I did, however, want to mention one other well-spring of ideas and feedback that you may find invaluable, now available to you as a campground owner: Twenty Group membership. A peer-to-peer approach adopted most prominently by manufacturers, Twenty Groups bring together up to 20 non-competing representatives of the same industry to share ideas, analyze each other's performances and help each other set performance goals. ARVC and KOA both sponsor Twenty Groups for their members, with each group rotating its semiannual meetings among the members' campgrounds; meetings typically run 2-3 days and include a critique of the host facility, as well as an annual deep dive into members' financial records for the previous year.

Twenty Groups aren't for everyone: despite vows of confidentiality, some campground owners are reluctant to share sensitive financial information. Because members come from all corners of the U.S. and even Canada, the twice-a-year meetings require more of a time and financial commitment than many campground owners are willing to expend. And while a well-run Twenty Group—the groups are all self-administered—can be an eye-opening experience for its participants, there's always the possibility for it to devolve into the cliques and interpersonal drama that can afflict any small group.

For all that, however, the potential payoff is enormous and worth checking out—if you're a KOA franchisee or ARVC member, that is.   ✑

Afterword

IF YOU'VE READ THIS FAR, the one lasting impression I hope I've left with you is that the private campground industry has become an extraordinarily dynamic place in which to gain a foothold. That means it has enormous potential payoffs—as attested by the number and speed with which investors are jumping in—but that comes at a high personal price, as operating a commercial RV park is a hugely demanding business. But that's not the end of it. These days, buying and then operating a campground also comes with unprecedented levels of risk.

As I write these concluding words, in mid-May, the challenges confronting everyone in the business include environmental, financial and economic threats that are getting only worse. Continued drought and escalating temperatures in the western states already have contributed to the largest wildfire in New Mexico's history, are draining Lake Powell and Lake Mead and have encroached on the Great Plains, with extensive grassfires scorching Kansas and Nebraska. Rising interest rates are ending a decade of easy money, which means buying a campground is becoming more costly with each passing month. And the war in Ukraine, coupled with ongoing global supply-chain disruptions caused by the pandemic, have pushed the price of oil to historic highs and made it increasingly more expensive for RVers to hit the road.

Yet despite all those headwinds, the flood of investor money continues unabated, and as a result, asking prices for campgrounds and RV parks are unsustainably high. The deep-pocketed interests willing to meet those prices can take care of themselves, but the odds are that you can't. Buying into a speculative bubble, as a lot of home buyers learned starting in 2006, invariably ends badly for the little guy. And while I understand the fear of being left behind—the overwhelming impulse to jump onto the train before it leaves the station—I'm urging you to tamp it down and get a grip. You have far too much to lose, and take it from me: this train will be back.

To the extent that some of the pressure to jump into the market is coming from headlines and self-promoters nattering on about industry consolidation and the rate at which campgrounds are being snapped up, it may help to put things in context. Yes, a handful of major players is assembling portfolios of two to three dozen campgrounds each and making waves by promoting new RV parks of 300 or more sites, but all that represents just a sliver of an incredibly large, varied and unconsolidated universe of camping facilities. It's going to take many years—if ever—for the campground industry to resemble its hotel counterpart, where a handful of major chains now dominate the landscape, which means there will be many more opportunities for independent campground ownership.

Less than a year ago, when I was wrapping up *Renting Dirt*, I wrote in the afterword how no one had a good handle on the commercial campground sector—not how many there were, nor how many RV sites they were offering or to what extent those sites were pull-throughs or had 50-amp pedestals. I quoted a 2020 report by CHM Government Services, which had been commissioned by the National Park Service to recommend how it could improve its public campgrounds, lamenting the dearth of reliable information about the private sector. "There is no equivalent of Smith Travel Research, a data aggregator for the lodging industry, for the private sector campground industry," CHM observed.

Fast forward ten months, and CHM Government Services has filled the breach itself. Retained by the RV Industry Association in an effort to finally get an idea of where the 600,000 RVs its members are manufacturing each year can go to camp, CHM concluded that the U.S. has 12,290 private campgrounds—roughly midway between industry estimates that ranged from 9,921 to 13,883. Of those, 12,118 can accommodate RVs and have 1.4 million sites among them. There are, in other words, a lot of campgrounds out there, and a lot of them will be getting sold each year for quite a few years to come.

So the opportunity to buy a campground, if less than ideal today, will rise and fall over time and your best chance will present itself eventually; just be patient.

The other parting thought I want to share is to recall the three primary rules of thumb for operating a campground that I mentioned at different points in the book, but not all in one place:

• You have to be there.

• Don't fix things that aren't broken—there are plenty of broken things waiting to be fixed.

• Under-promise and over-deliver, not the other way around.

Truth be told, the last two points are applicable to any small business, and especially one that caters to the public. But the first point, while also widely applicable, is absolutely crucial to the successful operation of a small or medium-sized camp-ground—something, I think, that the RV park consolidators haven't fully appreciated. From what I've seen, the single biggest limiting factor on how many properties an investor can acquire and oper-ate successfully is not money, but the lack of sufficiently trained and motivated management personnel. There just aren't enough campground managers who understand the business, have a suf-ficiently broad skill set and attention to detail, and have the pas-sion and drive to put in the hours needed to make a campground shine.

That's where you, as an owner-operator, will have a com-petitive edge. That's where you'll end up successfully tilling the soil, turning dirt, to produce a personal harvest that the corporate/ industrialized campground ventures can only dream about.

* * * * *

Finally, two parting notes. One, I want to acknowledge my wife, Carin, and sister, Ann, for proofreading my manuscript and for being my sounding boards as I developed it. Neither, it should go without saying, are responsible for any surviving errors of fact, construction, grammar or spelling, all of which are on me. Thank you both!

And second, I'd like readers to respond with their own thoughts and experiences, so any subsequent editions of *Turning Dirt* can be strengthened by your feedback. This is, after all—and as I've repeatedly emphasized—a fast-changing industry. Suggested additions, corrections or deletions can be sent to me at *azipser@ renting-dirt.com*. More of my writing about RVs and campgrounds can be read at my blog, *www.renting-dirt.com*.

Thanks—and good luck!

Appendix A

Sample offer letter
(suggested language only)

Dear Prospective Seller,

I/we are pleased to present you with the following terms for purchase of your campground, Sultry Pines Campground and RV Park.

Property: Sultry Pines Campground and RV Park in Any County, Blessed State, is a 180-site campground located on approximately 300 acres and includes all sites, cabins, storage facilities, equipment, and personal and intellectual property currently used to operate the business.

Purchase Price: $4.2 million

Seller Financing: Seller shall carry a note in the amount of $2 million at an interest rate of 4.5% and an amortization rate of 25 years. The seller note shall be subordinate to senior lender financing.

Inspection Period: Buyer or buyer's agent shall have 60 days to fully inspect the property and its financial and business records commencing on the date a purchase and sale agreement is signed.

Contingencies: *Due Diligence*: This offer is contingent upon Buyer's satisfactory review of the property, including but not limited to:

- Phase I environmental testing (Phase II if necessary)
- Confirmation of title/ownership
- Evaluation of all on-site utilities, infrastructure, equipment, and improvements
- Three years of financial records, including income tax returns, that confirm the business's revenue and expenses

Financing: This offer is contingent upon Buyer's ability to finance the purchase price at terms that are reasonable and acceptable to Buyer at Buyer's sole discretion. Buyer will use best efforts to achieve such financing.

Closing: The target closing date shall occur 30 days following the end of the inspection period, at which time the Seller shall deliver the property to Buyer free of any liens or encumbrances. To the extent desired by Buyer, Seller shall assist with management of the campground for up to two weeks following the closing date. Purchase price allocations shall be determined by Buyer and Seller prior to closing.

Binding Nature: The parties shall negotiate in good faith and on an exclusive basis to enter into a definitive sale and purchase agreement on or before the thirtieth day after this offer letter has been signed by both parties. This offer letter is intended to bind both Buyer and Seller to its terms, but the parties acknowledge that additional terms not described in this offer may be negotiated into the final agreement.

If this offer is acceptable to Seller, please sign below and return an original copy to Buyer by 5 p.m. on such-and-such a date, after which time the terms and conditions above shall be automatically withdrawn and be null and void without further action by Buyer.

Appendix B

Due diligence checklist

Things you should do and Items you should request and review during your due diligence period, understanding that not all campgrounds will have all the information listed.

Financials:
• Three years of tax returns, confirming revenue figures shown in previously reviewed P&Ls.
• Occupancy reports for past three years, showing usage by site type.
• Reservations report for current year vs. previous year-to-date, together with a list of advance deposits (to be updated just prior to closing).
• Summary of what taxes have been paid, including sales, real estate, and property taxes, as well as occupancy taxes (if any).

Operations:
• Conduct a municipal lien search and check for any outstanding violations.
• Copies of any leases, waivers or contracts with guests or storage customers.
• Copies of all customer rules and policies.
• Copies of all service or municipal agreements for water, sewer, garbage or other utilities or services.
• A list of store vendors and contact information.
• A list of marketing and website vendors, include internet hosting service, highway signage, and advertising contracts.
• Copies of any digital and physical marketing tools, such as logos, photographs, rack cards and site maps.
• Copies of all current insurance policies.
• Copies of all current licenses and permits, including

building permits, environmental operating permits, dump station permits, propane permits, and liquor, beer, wine, and food service licenses, if any. Find out which will transfer to a new owner, and which will require a renewed application.

• Copies of titles to all "vehicles," which may include RV camper rentals and park models.

Infrastructure:

• Any building plans, site plans or plat maps the campground may have. Lacking these, annotated drawings or maps of the park locating all buildings, sites, and utilities.

• An inventory of all cabins by age, make and model.

• A description of the swimming pool, including age, most recent refurbishing, and pump, disinfection and filtration systems.

• If the campground is on its own well and septic system, detailed information on each, including age, a map of septic tanks and field distribution systems, and contact information for the well driller and septic and well maintenance providers.

• A description of regular testing required by the Health Department or other governing agency, including pool and waterworks tests, together with record-keeping and reporting requirements. Review past test results.

• Physically inspect all equipment, utilities, buildings, amenities, and other improvements, such as roads, fences and sheds.

• Assess tree canopy and get a tree-trimming quote.

Staff:

• A list of all employees, including initial hire dates and current wages.

• A list of unfilled positions.

• Copies of employment contracts (if any) plus all employee handbooks and employee policies and procedures.

Appendix C

Elements of a purchase agreement

A campground purchase contract may vary considerably in appearance from one transaction to another, depending on who has prepared it and the controlling state or local jurisdiction, but certain elements will be common to almost all. These include the following:

• A summary of the parties to the transaction and a brief description of what is being sold and purchased, including not just the physical assets—land, buildings, equipment, etc.—but such paper assets as plans, operating manuals, warranties, and assignable titles and permits. A detailed equipment list, broken down building by building, should be appended to the contract.

• A statement of the financial terms and conditions of the purchase, including purchase price, down payment and terms and amount of bank financing. If there is to be seller financing, this also will be described, including the amount, amortization period, interest rate.

• A deadline for acceptance—coincident with the end of a defined inspection or "due diligence" period—and a closing date.

• A detailed description of the inspection period, outlining the buyer's (and his representatives') right of access to the property, as well as the documents and financial records the seller shall make available. These may include any property surveys, the existing title policy, all service and supply contracts, any environmental and engineering reports, all licenses and permits required for the business, and three years of the seller's business income tax returns and year-end statements.

• An itemized assignment of closing costs to the buyer and seller.

• A description of proration procedures, including a list of transactions and items to be prorated.

• A statement on whether the contract may be assigned to a third party, and if so, under what circumstances.

• A description of remedies if either the buyer or the seller will be in material default of the agreement.

• A description of contingencies that will void the contract without penalty to the buyer, including an unrectified title defect; the buyer's inability to secure bank financing despite a good-faith effort; or the seller's failure to provide a full and accurate accounting of the property's business records. Additional contingencies may include unsatisfactory results from a Phase I environmental study or a failure to agree on purchase price allocation.

• If the purchase includes seller financing, a seller's right to review buyer's financial statement and credit report.

• A requirement that the seller shall assist the buyer as an unpaid consultant and trainer for two weeks from the date of closing, as well as an additional period of several days to assist with winterizing or dewinterizing; in addition, the seller should be available for phone consultation for up to a year after closing.

• A statement that assigns risk of loss from damage to the property prior to the closing to the seller, and a requirement that the property be maintained and operated at the same level as before the sale.

• Assignment to the buyer of the right to continue using the campground's trade name, telephone numbers and website and email addresses.

Depending on specific circumstances, there also may be contract provisions addressing brokers' commissions, franchise transfers or a non-compete clause, barring the seller from working for a competing campground within a certain radius. There also may be additional provisions regarding seller financing, including prepayment penalties or interest rate adjustments at defined intervals.

Author's bio

BOOK-WRITING CONVENTION suggests it's appropriate for me to stick a note at the very tail end of anything I've written to let you, the reader, know who I am and why you should give some credence to what I have to say. So, most briefly:

Prior to owning an RV park and campground in the Shenandoah Valley for eight years (as detailed in my first book, *Renting Dirt*), our family lived in Manassas, VA while I worked as editor of *The Guild Reporter*, a now defunct publication of The Newspaper Guild, a labor union. Earlier in my career I had been a reporter, columnist and editor for a variety of small, medium and major newspapers, many of which also are no longer with us. I do not take any responsibility for their demise.

During those years I spent much time backpacking, both in the Mountain West and in the Appalachians, and our little family did a modest amount of RVing in pop-ups, small trailers, and Class Cs. Once we owned a campground and I was able to leave its operation to my family for a month each winter, I also took extensive overseas hiking trips in New Zealand, Tasmania, Nepal, Bhutan, Peru and Patagonia. The last is as close to heaven on earth as I can imagine, but then again, I like wind.

Since retiring from active campground management I've been maintaining a blog about all things RVing, *renting-dirt.com*, to which I post approximately twice a week, and have contributed erratically to *RVtravel*, an online RV publication. *Turning Dirt* is my second book on the subject, but now that I've corralled the "dirt" brand, I'm thinking my next effort should be titled *Dishing Dirt*. Could be fun. Send suggestions. Stay tuned.